Getting the Buggers to Turn Up

D0257073

Also available in the series

Sue Cowley: *Getting the Buggers to Behave 2*

Sue Cowley: *Getting the Buggers to Write*

Sue Cowley: *Getting the Buggers to Think*

Sue Cowley: *Letting the Buggers be Creative*

Mike Ollerton: *Getting the Buggers to Add Up*

Barbara Ward: *Getting the Buggers to Draw*

Amanda Barton: *Getting the Buggers into Languages*

Related titles

Alma Harris and Jane McGregor (Editors): **Improving Schools series**

Michael Marland and Rick Rogers: *How to be a Successful Form Tutor*

Susan Tranter and Adrian Percival: *How to Run your School Successfully*

Chris Turner: *How to Run Your Department Successfully*

Getting the Buggers to Turn Up

Ian McCormack

continuum
LONDON • NEW YORK

Continuum International Publishing Group

The Tower Building   15 East 26th Street
11 York Road   New York
London SE1 7NX   NY 10010

www.continuumbooks.com

© Ian McCormack 2005

All rights reserved. No part of this publication may be reproduced or transmitted in any form or by any means, electronic or mechanical, including photocopying, recording, or any information storage or retrieval system, without prior permission in writing from the publishers.

British Library Cataloguing-in-Publication Data
A catalogue record for this book is available from the British Library.

ISBN: 0–8264–7332–6 (paperback)

Typeset by BookEns Ltd, Royston, Herts.
Printed and bound in Great Britain by CPI Bath

BATH SPA UNIVERSITY
COLLEGE
NEWTON PARK LIBRARY

Class No.
371.5 MACC

Phil Dutch

Contents

Acknowledgements

My thanks are due to a large number of people who have assisted me in the writing of this book. Many of them are named and quoted in the text and I hope that their inclusion is both a mark of my gratitude and gives some indication of the value I attach to their opinions and their support.

Additionally, and in particular, there are some people that I would like to mention who have given me particular support or who have offered advice and for one reason or another are not mentioned in the text. My first thanks must go to Marcia and Kate who always, through their love and actions, give me endless encouragement and support. I would also like to thank Lizzie Gorman, Stephen Lawrence, Governor at Her Majesty's Young Offenders Institution, Appleton Thorn and Jenny Skean-Gillies in the Education Psychology Department at the same establishment, Phil McTague and everyone else at South Bromsgrove Community High School, Jonathan Potter and his colleagues in the Education Welfare Department in Warrington, Richard Foster of Wigan MBC Education Support Services, Peter Heath of Worcestershire and Herefordshire Youth Offending Service and Neil Monks for his computer wizardry.

Lastly, and by no means least, I must offer my thanks to the staff at Continuum, particularly Christina Parkinson for keeping in touch and most definitely Alexandra Webster for giving me the chance to do this work and for her advice and encouragement during its creation. If, after all of that, there is anyone I have forgotten please accept my apologies and of course my belated thanks.

Introduction

When teachers reach stress overload, as they so often do these days, there seem to be fewer and fewer places to turn. It is no surprise, or at least no surprise to those who work in the classroom, that some colleagues go through the exit door rather than continuing the seemingly endless search for solutions to the equally endless stream of problems.

The surprise for most teachers comes after they leave the classroom and they discover that their skills are in demand. Trained teachers, despite what we are told, are blessed with a range of skills that are highly valued in the world at large. Organization, management, interpersonal skills, initiative, decision-making and flexibility are just a few of the skills used on a regular basis by teachers in a classroom situation. It is the intention of this book to make use of those skills and to apply them to the improvement of attendance in schools.

In the final analysis education is a product like any other and, as teachers, we use our skills to 'sell' ideas to those in our care. Hopefully, in the process we inspire in the learners the same love for learning that we have. Failing that we are nevertheless satisfied if we are able to make some sort of difference and our pupils can take away something that will serve them positively at some point in the future.

For the most part we are very successful in this quest, but there is no doubt that in a small but significant number of cases, we signally fail in our attempts. Either the pupils are not there to learn in the first place or, over a period of time, they opt out by not attending or by absenting themselves mentally from the learning process.

It is the behaviour of these children and our reaction to them that this book sets out to address. From the outset it is important to recognize that the author has no illusions about creating and offering ready-made solutions to every problem that exists. Not only would that be impossible, it would also be insulting to the professionalism and judgement of colleagues who deal with attendance on a daily basis. What this book can do, however, is explore the phenomenon of truancy and offer flexible strategies that colleagues can apply to their own specific problems.

Avoiding the use of academic jargon, it is the author's intention to give practical and accessible advice to teachers without unduly increasing their existing workload. This book offers definitions, extends understanding of non-attendance, educates colleagues (thereby enlisting their help), offers insights into the views of parents and informs management of the level of support they should be offering to the staff charged with improving attendance.

It is likely that only a handful of the ideas offered will prove useful, and in only a limited number of cases. Nevertheless, it is the fervent hope of the author that the ideas offered will, when combined with the professional skills of the reader, increase the ability to deal with the difficult problem of attendance.

Education is rarely about miracles: it is more often about making small but significant differences to the lives of the pupils in our care. If, in the final analysis, we can look back and feel that we have communicated with those previously outside the education system and allowed them access to choices, information and opportunities that might otherwise have passed them by, we will have started to make that 'small difference'.

Ian McCormack
May 2004

1 Why Address the Problem?

Why are we trying to alter behaviour?

'Education matters to people. It is more than just a public service and provides the very basis for a fulfilled life and a civilized society.'

These words, from Charles Clarke, Secretary of State for Education and Skills, open his introduction to the DfES booklet: *Education and Skills: The Economic Benefits* (available for downloading at www.dfes.gov.uk).

He goes on to say:

' ... in a rapidly expanding global economy the value of education and skills cannot be overestimated. The future prosperity of the country depends upon our collective knowledge and skills ... '

The views expressed in the booklet are unequivocal. A failure to educate *the entire* nation places a burden upon the whole of society.

What are the economic facts?

'Highly educated people are more productive. That is why they earn more and are more likely to be employed.'

Research has shown that there is a clear link between earnings and qualifications. Indeed for high earners the level of the reward they receive is more closely linked to their qualifications than to their particular skills or ability.

Education gives choice

A qualified and trained employee need never be obliged to accept less for their labour since they should be able to receive a better rate of pay with a different employer. By the same token, and this is the problem facing the non-attender, no sensible or honest employer will ever pay more to a worker than that worker's qualifications or training are capable of producing. The inevitable link between these facts and long-term employment are presented in Figure 1.1.

Truancy is expensive

There can be no doubt that truancy is expensive. OECD (Organization for Economic and Cultural Development) figures in 2002 revealed that 20 per cent of the 16–65 age group in the UK were at or below the accepted level for basic literacy. These figures placed the UK behind many of its major competitors. Given the proven link between education, wage levels and employment prospects there can be no doubt that the non-attender is far more likely to become (and remain throughout their lifetime) a burden to the nation's benefit system than the successful student who has achieved choice through education and training.

British Government figures relating to crime add weight to this argument and the author's research (albeit using a small sample) confirm the eventual costs of truancy in terms of crime, unemployment, imprisonment and subsequent rehabilitation.

Education, truancy, crime and health

Research by the Scottish Council for Research in Education across seven English LEAs found that in addition to academic underachievement there were significant links between truancy, crime, stress and other social problems such as premature sexual activity and rates of teenage pregnancy. The British Government's booklet *Education and Skills: The Economic Benefits* supports this view and asserts:

> 'There is a wealth of evidence linking education with outcomes such as better health, longer life expectancy, lower infant mortality and reduced crime.'

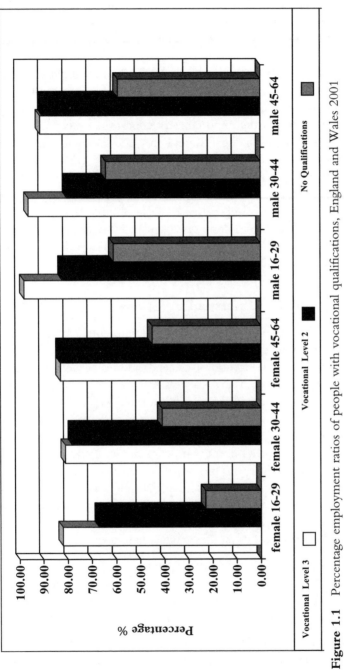

Figure 1.1 Percentage employment ratios of people with vocational qualifications, England and Wales 2001
(Labour force survey, winter 2001.)

Referring to a number of reports and research programmes, the booklet goes on to say that the incidence of good health is twice as likely amongst the better educated, and that mortality rates amongst the adult population are closely linked to occupational group and hence levels of education. Whilst in some cases other factors may have influenced these findings, other research linking good numeracy skills to a reduction in long-term health problems seems to establish the importance of educational success.

Research in both the UK and the US has established links between truancy and delinquency. Indeed, in the US, research has demonstrated that not only does high school graduation significantly reduce criminal activity, but that very early success in education is also important. Pre-school attendance, it seems, particularly for those from disadvantaged backgrounds, results eventually in less involvement in criminal damage, less need for remedial help, more success at school and higher earnings.

The problem of persuading others

Despite the strength of the economic arguments it is sometimes difficult to apply the national picture to individual cases of truancy that are affecting the school in general, and other well-motivated pupils in particular. Many teachers feel, with some justification, that their job is difficult enough without taking responsibility for the long-term employment prospects of difficult pupils or for reducing the proportion of public money spent by the Benefits Agency. Given their current workloads and budgetary constraints, schools concentrate on the problems that immediately affect them, feeling that they have neither the time nor the resources to deal with wider issues. Even though the proportion of persistent truants is low in most schools pragmatism, born out of necessity, often leads teachers to an inevitable conclusion:

> '. . . staff seem to feel that they spend a disproportionate amount of time either implementing procedures to encourage good attendance or dealing with the consequences of poor attendance.' (SCRE report 'Absence from Schools' May 2003.)

Whilst this may well be true there are other costs associated with truancy that schools must consider. If the encouragement of good attendance is expensive, re-admission processes are even more costly. Truants who return to school demand more attention so that they can catch up. Many regular attenders resent this and become de-motivated themselves, presenting the teacher with another set of challenges relating to the school's performance statistics.

The SCRE research programme quoted above found that

> ' ... teachers try to help truants catch up but feel frustrated in their efforts; schools fear the loss of their reputations; and secondary pupils were able to study better when truants were not in class ... the effects were ... most noticeable in schools with large numbers of poor attenders [where] the issues of how to deal with absence and behaviour management become intermingled.'

Why are truants deserving of help and resources?

Clearly unless steps are taken to address the problem then it will become more, not less costly. Young offenders interviewed by the author, and discussed in some detail in Chapter 5, despite being alienated from the school process, were nevertheless clear about what they felt should have been provided and what might have changed their attitude to education. Repeatedly the same concerns were voiced in interviews.

Feeling wanted

For many of those interviewed this was a recurrent theme. Many talked about the atmosphere of judgement that they felt in schools. They knew they couldn't do things or that they came from different backgrounds to many of the other pupils, but what they wanted to feel was not judgement but interest. Without fail the interviewees believed they had succeeded best when they felt time had been set aside for them so that they could work in smaller groups and feel valued.

Safety at school

Many of those interviewed cited fear or uncertainty in the school environment as a starting point for their non-attendance or their behavioural difficulties. Since many were largely inarticulate they had responded by choosing either 'fight or flight', and both choices had, in effect, achieved the same result: conflict with the school system. The development of a safe environment in school will be dealt with in Chapter 7.

Parental liaison and monitoring attendance

These issues were clearly connected to the concerns voiced about safety and feeling valued. Discussions with truants frequently revealed that in their view ' ... they [the school] didn't care ... they never checked up and they never told your parents'.

Though not universally true, some of the young offenders did feel that had these procedures been in place they might have thought twice about their spontaneous decisions to truant, and that had they done so things might have been different. This view is borne out in the SCRE report already referred to in this chapter, which reports on page 61 that ' ... pupils establish habits [of truancy] earlier in their school careers which they find hard to break'.

Liaison with other agencies

Although there can be no doubt that truancy is expensive and that poverty is a contributory factor, it cannot simply be measured in monetary terms and its causes cannot be blithely attributed to one issue. The circumstances surrounding the truancy of the young offenders interviewed by the author included substance abuse, inappropriate behaviour, violence, and lack of interest in courses. Since schools are unlikely to have all of the expertise available to deal with these issues then the answer would seem to be the development of a multi-agency approach which would both develop the curriculum and address some of the budgetary problems. This course of action will be examined further in Chapter 6.

The educational perspective

Despite the very strong economic evidence related to truancy, not all of the reasons for intervention are so unashamedly extrinsic in their make up. Education is not simply about pounds and pennies. Few teachers (if any) entered the teaching profession intent upon reducing public sector borrowing or hoping to increase the gross domestic product.

Teachers are teachers because they love their chosen subjects. They have experienced the choice and enrichment that education has given to them, they find personal fulfilment in offering that chance to others and they want to make a difference, on a personal basis, to the lives of the young people in their care.

On the basis of these reasons alone there is a strong argument for attempting both to alter the behaviour of the truant and to offer them access to wider educational opportunity. As educators we cannot simply discard people because they are unprepared to 'buy in' unconditionally to our values, however much those values might mean to us. Though the frustration that teachers experience when faced with a frequently absent or disruptive pupil is entirely understandable, to simply dismiss those pupils who reject what we have to offer is a denial of the vocation that we claim as teachers.

Although it might not reflect every facet of the truth, what we must do is accept that irrespective of other factors there are two basic reasons why the truant rejects school.
Either:

- There is something wrong with our message

Or:

- There is something wrong with the way in which we are seeking to communicate our message

Since we are dealing with individuals this view will, without doubt, present us with as many problems as there are truants in the school, but this, in many respects, is the name of the game. We are the professionals. We are the people who have set ourselves up as authorities. We have studied our subjects. We have experience, backed up by a plethora of research and statistics. The truant has nothing. We are the ones who have to change and develop strategies to address the problems because we are the ones equipped to do so.

Figure 1.2, though not a definitive profile, will, nevertheless, give an idea of some of the lifestyle issues experienced by the truant. If we can say without fear or favour that we would be happy

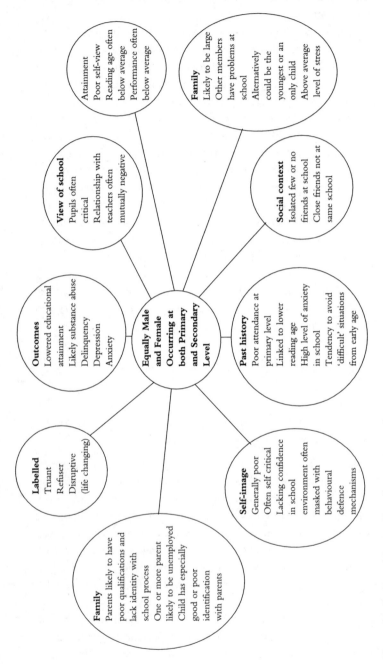

Attainment
Poor self-view
Reading age often
below average
Performance often
below average

Family
Likely to be large
Other members
have problems at
school
Alternatively
could be the
youngest or an
only child
Above average
level of stress

View of school
Pupils often
critical
Relationship with
teachers often
mutually negative

Social context
Isolated few or no
friends at school
Close friends not at
same school

Outcomes
Lowered educational
attainment
Likely substance abuse
Delinquency
Depression
Anxiety

**Equally Male
and Female
Occurring at
both Primary
and Secondary
Level**

Past history
Poor attendance at
primary level
Linked to lower
reading age
High level of anxiety
in school
Tendency to avoid
'difficult' situations
from early age

Labelled
Truant
Refuser
Disruptive
(life changing)

Self-image
Generally poor
Often self critical
Lacking confidence
in school
environment often
masked with
behavioural
defence
mechanisms

Family
Parents likely to have
poor qualifications and
lack identity with
school process
One or more parent
likely to be unemployed
Child has especially
good or poor
identification
with parents

Figure 1.2 Possible profile of an individual absentee

imposing such a personality profile on any of the young people in our care then the problem is solved. We need do no more. The truant has no need of our help and we have no mandate to offer it. If however, as is more likely, we conclude that this is a situation to which we must respond then we must continue in our attempts to understand truancy and we must make strenuous attempts to prevent its occurrence.

What outcomes are we aiming to achieve?

The decision that a school takes about outcomes for any attendance project will, inevitably, vary according to the particular circumstances of each establishment. On the face of it the simple answer to the question is that we should seek to get 100 per cent of children attending school 100 per cent of the time. However, given that truancy levels have remained constant since national data was first recorded and acknowledging the fact that the British Government failed in its target to reduce truancy by a third in 2002, the target of complete eradication of truancy would seem, in the short term at least, to be somewhat unrealistic. (British Government targets have been amended and now aim for 'the reduction of 2002 truancy levels by ten per cent in 2004'.)

In conferring 'Truancy Buster Awards' in 2001 the DfEE (as it then was) acknowledged the difference in school circumstances by recognizing schools who had achieved success but had done so at markedly different levels. Some were rewarded for maintaining low levels of absence whilst others were rewarded for percentage differences ranging from 0.1 per cent to 9.3 per cent. In short the answer must be that schools must review their own circumstances and, in consultation with other agencies such as the LEA, the Education Welfare Service (EWS) and the police, decide on targets and time scales that are appropriate to their circumstances.

At the same time, those responsible for the management of attendance in schools should acknowledge the ambivalence felt by some staff towards attempts to improve the attendance of certain pupils. In the view of some staff, the absence of these students enhances the classroom atmosphere and gives the well-motivated pupils greater opportunities to succeed. Whilst this point of view is often demonstrably true, it fails to acknowledge the broader issues associated with attendance. In the first place, if the well-motivated pupil has the right to succeed, so too do those who are, for whatever reason, currently de-motivated.

Equally, though it might seem that the absence of certain pupils is improving the performance of others, and consequently that of the school, in truth this is not the case. In 2001, when launching the British Government's attendance policies as Secretary of State for Education, Estelle Morris clarified the situation when she pointed out that absent pupils remain on the school roll and thus that 'Absent children negate all other work by reducing the school's achievement'.

She went on to say:

'On this basis it is in a school's interest to develop strategies that will keep children in school thus allowing the school and the pupils to achieve results that would otherwise have been lost.'

That then must be a school's target, to bring pupils back into school and, in doing so, offer them opportunities to succeed that previously might not have been available to them. By taking this approach and devising an alternative curriculum not only will the motivated pupils be allowed to continue with their studies unhindered, but the disaffected will also be able to achieve and, in the long term, the culture of truancy will be eroded.

How do we measure success?

From the detailed examination of alternative courses and attendance strategies made in later sections it will be clear that the improvement of attendance in schools and the measurement of that improvement is far from straightforward. In terms of recording absence, schools must take note of the points made in Chapter 2 and follow a standardized process for recording and classifying absence. Without such a baseline it will be impossible to calculate success at even the most rudimentary level.

At the same time as evaluating statistics, schools will have to evaluate the initiatives that they choose to put into place. This requirement must be acknowledged at the planning stage and, as with any development plan, there must be a process of development, implementation, evaluation and modification. The nature of the initiatives will often determine the criteria for success, but colleagues must be made aware that levels of success may be very small at first and that it is a change in culture that we are working towards rather than instant transformations. In the first instance, for example, encouraging a non-attender to come to school on a part-time basis must be viewed as a step forward.

There will, inevitably, be other members of the school community who will be uneasy about the idea of treating some pupils differently but the fact is that the non-attender *is* different, presenting different challenges and demanding different solutions. In this way non-attenders are no different to children with dyslexia, gifted and talented children, children coping with bereavement or any other child with special needs who schools deal with on a daily basis.

If we fail to respond to the needs of the truant then we have failed in our duty to offer inclusive education to all members of the school community. Such a failure, given the available statistics, will affect the pupils concerned for the rest of their lives.

Conclusion

Above all, the evidence to come out of research into truancy is that it is immensely costly both to the individual and to society at large. Young people who truant are more likely to be involved in crime, often as the victims, and their chances of achieving academic success and good social skills are damaged. They are more likely to be unemployed, in all probability will become young parents and, in doing so, may well create the next generation of truants. Society has to address the problem and schools must be central to the solution. In an interview with the author Jonathan Potter, Principal Education Welfare Officer for Warrington in Cheshire, summed up the approach we should expect from schools:

'How we respond to this group (those absent without acceptable excuse) is a measure of our commitment to building supportive school communities which foster high achievement for all students.'

2 Truancy: Legal Implications

The legal definition

When we begin to define truancy it becomes apparent, almost immediately, that we are not dealing with a single activity but with a range of behaviours, and that the lines between each are somewhat blurred. It is essential therefore that any school or local authority preparing policies to improve attendance should be aware of the problems of definition and should take them and the different motives for truancy into account.

Different types of truancy are examined in more detail in Chapter 3. However, in extreme cases, where a child fails to attend school, irrespective of school contact, the intervention of the Education Welfare Service (EWS) or even the direction of the courts ensures there can be little doubt that truancy is taking place and that the child's parents are breaking the law. In such clear-cut cases it is reasonable to turn to the law for a definition. Section 16 of the Crime and Disorder Act 1998, Subsection (4) states:

> 'A child's or young person's absence from a school shall be taken to be without lawful authority unless it falls within subsection (3) (leave, sickness, unavoidable cause or days set aside for religious observance) of Section 444 of the Education Act 1996.'

The legal position for parents

The prime responsibility for ensuring that children attend school rests with the parents. Section 7 of the Education Act 1996 clearly states that the parent is responsible for ensuring that children of compulsory school age receive an education that is 'suitable to the child's age, ability and aptitude and to any special education needs the child may have'. This can be achieved through regular attendance at a local authority school or through some other process. The parent might, for example, elect to send a child to an independent school or to provide education in the home environment.

However, if a child fails to attend school then the parent must work closely and actively with the school and the EWS to resolve the situation. Failure by a parent to cooperate can lead to prosecution. The possible outcomes of such a course of action are included below in the section headed 'Sanctions'. Further information for parents can be found in the DfES leaflet 'Is Your Child Missing Out on School Attendance? Information for Parents'. This leaflet, which was updated in 2002, is published in English and seventeen community languages and is available for distribution to parents. It can be obtained from the DfES by quoting reference PPY 181.

What is meant by compulsory school age?

The Education Act of 1996 (details available on the DfES attendance website) defines compulsory school age as beginning from the age of five. A child must attend school from the start of the term commencing on or after his/her fifth birthday. Compulsory education must then continue until the last Friday of June in the school year that the child reaches 16 years of age.

The legal position for schools

The governing body

The governing body of the school is legally responsible for the attendance register and must ensure that the school is registered with the Data Protection Registrar under the Data Protection Act of 1998. More advice can be obtained from the Office of the Data Protection Register (tel. 01625 545745) and further DfES guidance on registers in general is available online by following the links at www.dfes.gov.uk.

The headteacher

The law requires headteachers to ensure that accurate records of attendance are kept in their schools. The attendance register must be taken twice a day, once at the start of the morning session and once at some point during the afternoon session. The attendance register must accurately record the whereabouts of every child on the school roll. It must state whether the pupil is present in school or elsewhere as part of an approved educational activity (e.g. a field trip), or if he/she is absent. If a pupil is absent that absence must be recorded as either authorized or unauthorized.

If the school uses a computerized registration system then a hard copy must be printed out at least once a month. These monthly records must be bound into annual volumes and, like manual registers, must be kept for at least three years.

Each year every school is obliged to submit details of attendance figures to the DfES. These figures must indicate:

- How many half days were missed by pupils due to authorized absence
- How many half days were missed by pupils due to unauthorized absence

It is the responsibility of the headteacher to ensure that the school has a clear policy relating to attendance. It should include:

- Advice for parents on expectations regarding attendance
- The need for absence notes
- Procedures for contacting the school and informing them of an absence
- The consequences of non-attendance

When informing parents about the consequences of non-attendance the school should make the legal position clear. However, the central issue in all attendance policies should be the pupil. Therefore: emphasis should be placed on the welfare of the pupil in the hope that parents come to see attendance as a benefit and entitlement for their child that will ultimately provide opportunities and, in the long term, facilitate choice.

Pupils should also be aware of the school's policies, their own responsibilities and the possible outcomes due to non-attendance and all staff should be familiar with the content and administration of the attendance policy and must ensure that it is applied consistently.

It is up to the headteacher to ensure that all interested parties are informed of the attendance policy, that they are regularly reminded of its content and that they are consulted as part of periodic policy reviews.

How is truancy recorded?

In its 2003 report for the DfES, 'Absence From School. A Study of its Causes and Effects in Seven LEAs', the SCRE (Scottish Council for Research in Education) concluded that the variations in definition applied to truancy (see Chapter 3) and the different criteria applied by schools to categorize absence meant that ' ... few safe conclusions can be drawn about the extent of the absence problem or the efficacy of methods adopted to combat it'.

This view notwithstanding, it is possible for schools to draw conclusions from their own work provided that they employ a consistent approach to the application of their attendance policy and to the recording of absence and attendance. If in the recording of attendance statistics schools accurately follow the advice contained in Circular 10/99, 'Social Inclusion: Pupil Support' (available from DfES publications or at their website, www.dfes.gov.uk/schoolattendance), then the available statistics will become increasingly accurate and the conclusions drawn increasingly safe.

Recording attendance and absence
Schools may keep registers either manually or on computer and may, in consultation with their LEA and EWS, use a variety of codes to identify types and patterns of absence. However, schools must always differentiate between authorized and unauthorized absence and must make the distinction on the basis of advice contained in Annexe A of Circular 10/99. Further information and clarification can be found (via the DfES website quoted above) in the Crown Copyright document, Statutory Instrument 1995 No. 2098, 'The Education (Pupil Registration) Regulations 1995' (Amended 1997 and 2001).

Recording and categorizing attendance

Since 1997 there are four categories of attendance/absence:

- *Present*. Indicated by the use of a forward or reverse oblique line (either / or \).
- *Approved educational activity*. Indicated solely by the use of the appropriate code letter. No circle (O) is used with this category.
- *Authorized absence*. Indicated by the use of a circle (O) with the appropriate code letter inserted.
- *Unauthorized absence*. Indicated by the use of a circle (O) with no code letter inserted, apart from in the case of lateness after registration.

Suggested registration codes

As part of the move to standardize registration and thereby improve attendance, many schools have found it useful to use codes to identify types and patterns of absence. Although the DfES does not specify standard codes they do suggest that individual schools should be guided by the advice of their LEA. Schools using an electronic registration system can specify particular requirements and suppliers will usually install the appropriate codes when the system is set up or if subsequent revisions are required. Although broadly similar, the advice given by LEAs throughout England and Wales may differ slightly. The coding advice given to local authority schools by Warrington EWS is included below for illustrative purposes only, and individual schools should consult their own local authority to ensure the accuracy of the systems they adopt.

Approved educational activity No circle. Use only the appropriate code.	Code
Approved sporting activity	P
School visit or field trip	V
Work experience	W
Link courses with college or if pupils receive some part of their education 'off site'	Z
Pupil is attending another school/place of education and being registered there	B

Authorized absence **A circle (O) with the appropriate code letter inserted.**	**Code**
Absent for a 'performance' approved and licensed by the LEA	A
Special circumstances not covered by other codes	C
Exclusion: fixed term and permanent awaiting confirmation by governing body	E
Term-time family holiday, up to a maximum of ten school days	H
Interview	I
Illness/medically related	M
Day of religious observance	R
Study leave	S
Traveller absence (only if the child is expected to return)	T
Unauthorized Absence	O (no code)

Lateness	**Code**
Late within registration period or for an acceptable reason and therefore present	O with / or \ superimposed
Late after registration or without acceptable reason and therefore unauthorized absence	O with L inserted

N.B.: Whenever a code indicates that a pupil is 'off site' for some reason, schools should ensure that there is an adequate process for confirming the pupil's actual attendance. Without this process it is possible for pupils to use the school's systems to mask their absence.

Authorized absence

The authorization of absence is entirely a decision for the school and there is no obligation on the part of the school to accept an explanation if they do not think that it is accurate or if they feel it is insufficient to cover the full period of absence. In practical terms there are times when it is difficult to dispute a parental explanation and it may be more advisable to inform parents that the school will not accept such explanations on future occasions without additional evidence such as a medical note. Schools that make this policy clear in their attendance policy and through regular communication with parents find these situations easier to deal with. Schools that make it clear to parents that they will not automatically authorize absence often see a short-term reduction in unauthorized absence, and in the longer term experience an overall improvement in attendance.

Lateness

According to DfES advice on register codes pupils can be late before or after the closure of the register. In the latter case, if there is no satisfactory explanation, the lateness constitutes an unauthorized absence. Legal precedent dating back to 1961 states that if a child is regularly late then parents are failing to ensure 'efficient full-time education' and are, in consequence, committing an offence.

For the purposes of determining lateness the DfES advises that registers should remain 'open' for 30 minutes. The school's policy on lateness should be stated in the attendance policy and should be clearly communicated to parents on a regular basis.

Straightforward as all of this would appear to be, schools are nevertheless advised to use caution when dealing with lateness. Too severe an approach may well encourage children not too attend at all rather than face the consequences of lateness. On the other hand too relaxed an approach may well promote the idea that punctuality is unimportant. In arriving at a policy, it is a good idea for schools to remember that the pupils should be at the centre of any initiative. Though late for school a pupil will not necessarily be culpable and schools should take care to ensure that home circumstances are considered before action is taken. Those schools that involve the parents as well as the pupil when reacting to punctuality and that have a 'sliding scale' of sanctions, such as detentions proportionate to the amount of lateness, are likely to achieve the best results.

Internal lateness

This type of lateness is actually a form of 'near truancy' (see Chapter 3) and can, if it goes unchecked, prove to be extremely costly. A pupil who is five minutes late for every lesson could, conceivably, by the end of a week have missed approximately half a day's education. Whilst the situation might be easy to detect, particularly using an electronic system that tracks pupils in each lesson, the reasons may well be more complex and simply reacting by imposing punishment may not be the answer.

Term-time holidays

Whilst schools have the right of discretion when granting leave of absence for family holidays during term time, parents do not have the right to automatically withdraw their children. Once again this is an area that attracts some debate, and a school's response will depend on individual factors such as family circumstances, the length and timing of the holiday and a pupil's previous attendance record. Blanket policies of any sort are likely to be inappropriate and, should the matter result in any kind of formal appeal or legal proceedings, may be indefensible. Once again, schools will achieve the best results by keeping parents well-informed, outlining their policy and explaining the likely impact of term-time holidays on the continuity of a child's learning.

In exceptional circumstances schools can agree to an extended leave of absence over and above the normal period of ten school days. This provision is frequently relevant when ethnic minority families wish to return to their country of origin, and in some areas of the United Kingdom this can have a marked effect on the overall attendance figures. If a school does grant exceptional leave of absence then they should agree a return date in advance and ensure that parents understand the impact that such a decision may have upon a child's education. Schools should also be aware that in some cultures a return to the country of origin may be seen as part of a religious observance and not as a holiday. Under these and any other circumstances relating to the attendance and welfare of ethnic minority pupils, schools should ensure that where necessary an interpreter is available to ensure that all parties fully understand the situation.

Sanctions

If parents fail in their legal duty to ensure their child's attendance at school there are a number of steps which schools, LEAs and the police can take to ensure attendance. Some of the processes are voluntary and others can be enforced through prosecution and court order. However, LEAs and EWSs across England and Wales generally agree that prosecution should only be used if other processes have been exhausted. Indeed it is likely that courts will expect to see evidence of other support measures carried out by schools and local authorities before they will allow a prosecution to proceed.

Fast-track prosecutions
Notwithstanding the above, where the offence of Failing to Ensure School Attendance is persistent and families fail to respond to parenting contracts and other support mechanisms, legislation is now in place in England and Wales to enable fast-track prosecutions. These take place over a short period (usually twelve weeks) and are intended to give schools and LEAs the opportunity to deal quickly and decisively with acute attendance problems. Details of this system can be found in DfES document, 'Ensuring Regular School Attendance.' (See below under 'Legal Proceedings' for access details.)

School Attendance Order
If a child is not on the roll of a school the LEA is obliged by law to seek a School Attendance Order. This process is long and complicated and involves a series of letters and notices that must be served within a specific time scale. The application for an attendance order is usually made by the LEA and not by a school. It is most likely to be used when parents fail to register a child of compulsory school age, provide inadequate home education or are in dispute with the LEA about the school place allocated to their child.

Education Supervision Order
An Education Supervision Order (ESO) is likely to be used when parents are trying to ensure their child's attendance at school but are unsuccessful because of the child's attitude, emotional issues or some other barrier to their success. Under these circumstances the Education Welfare Officer must 'befriend' the child and the family and offer advice and assistance that will serve to address the problems. An ESO can only be effective if there is cooperation

from the parents, and where that is not present another course of action must be taken. LEAs must consider applying for an ESO before prosecuting a parent.

Parenting contracts
If a child fails to attend school the LEA or the governing body of the school may consider offering a parenting contract to the family. The contract is a formal written agreement between the governing body or the LEA and the parents and contains:

- A statement by the parents that they agree to comply, for a specified period, with whatever requirements are specified in the contract.
- A statement by the LEA or the governing body agreeing to supply support to the parent for the purpose of complying with the contract.

Parenting contracts are voluntary and there is obligation neither on the part of the school or LEA to offer a contract nor on the part of the parent to accept. However, such contracts have been found useful both in developing productive relationships between schools and parents and in identifying and addressing the underlying causes of non-attendance.

Parenting orders
Parenting orders consist of two elements:

- A requirement for the parent to attend counselling and guidance where they will receive help and support to enable them to improve their child's behaviour.
- A requirement to comply with the requirements of the order for up to twelve months.

Orders can be imposed in the case of non-attendance and exclusion. Parents failing to comply with such an order can be liable to a fine of up to £1000.

Penalty notices
Changes to the Anti-social Behaviour Act 2003 introduced two new sections allowing the imposition of penalty notices as an alternative to prosecution for failing to ensure attendance. The

fine is £50, rising to £100 if it is unpaid for 28 days. If the penalty is not paid in full after 42 days the LEA will normally prosecute the parent. If found guilty it is possible that the parent could face a term of imprisonment.

Under the new provisions penalty notices can be issued by:

- Authorized LEA staff.
- Headteachers and authorized school staff (limited to deputy and assistant heads) in line with LEA policy.
- The police, community support officers and accredited persons.

In June 2003 the first penalty notices were issued to 40 families across five education authorities in the Midlands and the North of England. It is intended that the scheme will operate across the whole of England by the end of 2004.

The Crime and Disorder Act (England and Wales) 1998

This legislation recognizes the link between anti-social behaviour and non-attendance at school. Within the legislation there is a variety of provisions that allow for dealing with truancy. The provisions of the act include:

- Truants caught in a public place may be removed from that place and returned to school or other designated premises.
- Pupils guilty of non-attendance may be made the subject of an Anti-social Behaviour Order.
- Parents of non-attenders may be prosecuted or made the subject of parenting orders.

This legislation is likely to be administered by the police, the Youth Offending Service, EWSs and other associated agencies.

Parenting courses

Largely in response to the Crime and Disorder Act (England and Wales) 1998, many local authorities perceived the need to provide effective parenting courses, and amongst the first to respond was Warrington, in the north-west of England. The scheme, largely devised by Sue Graham, Senior Education Welfare Officer for Warrington, was piloted as a joint initiative between Social

Services and the EWS. Sue says:

> 'The intention was (and still is) to provide a voluntary early intervention strategy for parents that would provide support for families and reduce the likelihood of Education Supervision Orders or Mandatory Parenting Orders.'

Participation

The school, social services, the EWS or some other statutory agency such as the GP or Education Psychologist can recommend participation in the course. The course is not designed to be a behaviour modification course: 'It is more', says Sue, 'about the process of change.' The course shows parents that they should start with the child and the needs of the child. It deals with aspects of communication including silent listening, reflective listening, positive communication, behaviour management and conflict resolution.

Having said that, behaviour modification is not the prime aim of the course, it is often an incidental outcome, for both parents and children.

Course content

During the course parents are encouraged to decide what they hope to achieve with their children and are asked to consider what changes and improvements they can make to achieve the desired outcome. A course takes, in total, fifteen hours spread over a ten-week period. Each session lasts for an hour and a half. The first and the last sessions, which take place in the home environment, are pre-course and post-course assessments. The remaining eight, which take place in a central location, are used to deliver the course content. In order to ensure access, the EWS arranges transport for all of the participants. Each week the course leader sets some sort of task or homework for the participants. The tasks are simple, easily achievable and do not depend on literacy skills. Their purpose is to maintain the clients' focus from week to week in order to ensure continuity. One of the main aims is to build the parents' confidence in order to deal with situations and in some cases to address issues related to their own parenting.

Evaluation
Since Warrington introduced the courses over three years ago feedback has been very positive. Attendance has been good and no parents have refused to participate. Schools have reported an improvement in attendance by the clients' children and the Behaviour Support Team has noted similarly positive outcomes. The EWS in Warrington has taken part in research conducted by the Institute of Education for the DfES. The findings (in 'Improving Children's Behaviour and Attendance through the use of Parenting Programmes: An Examination of Good Practice', Research Report 585, Institute of Education, University of London), indicate positive outcomes for attendance in the areas of the country where this and similar schemes have operated.

Running a course
In some areas similar courses have been organized by the Youth Offending Service using grants from the DfES BIP and BEST programmes (details available on www.dfes.gov.uk and in Chapter 6). Other local authorities have devised their own courses but, such has been the success of the Warrington model, it has been marketed nationally and is available through Continyou (www.continyou.org.uk), an education charity based in Coventry, England.

Legal proceedings

In the case of any prosecution, schools must seek the advice of the LEA and all other relevant agencies. All legal proceedings are governed by PACE (the Police and Criminal Evidence Act, 1984) and the correct procedures must be followed if the process is to be legal and effective.

Further details of this and all of the above measures are available in the following documents:

- Education Act 1996
- Children Act 1989
- Crime and Disorder Act 1998
- Ensuring Regular School Attendance: Guidance on the Legal Measures to Secure Regular School Attendance

All are available on the DfES website (www.dfes.gov.uk/
schoolattendance).

What are the current statistics?

In total, absence across primary and secondary schools amounts to
50,000 pupils missing school without permission every day. Over
one million pupils are involved in some sort of unauthorized
absence from school each year, equating to the loss of 1.1 per cent
of school days in secondary schools and 0.5 per cent of school
days in primary schools, and giving an average loss of 0.7 per cent
of school days across the two sectors. Truancy is not evenly spread
and figures for inner-city schools indicate a 33 per cent higher
incidence than the national average.

Pupil absence figures for schools in England in 2002/2003 are
shown in Appendix A.

3 Different Types of Truancy

Despite the legal definition offered in Chapter 2, it is nevertheless true that there are as many types of truancy as there are truants. It is a phenomenon defined not by the severity of the offence but by the participation of the pupil in that offence. To that extent at least the term 'truancy' is an explanatory fiction in that it seeks to define, in one word, a spectrum of different behaviours carried out by numerous individuals for a variety of reasons. In the 2003 report, 'Absence from School', the SCRE divides truancy into three distinct areas:

- *Truancy*. Described as absences that pupils acknowledged would be unacceptable to teachers. E.g.: deliberately missing lessons in order to avoid homework deadlines.
- *Unacceptable absences*. Described as absences that pupils knew would be unacceptable to teachers but were not seen as such by pupils. E.g.: pupils went out for family reasons or had stayed up late so decided to have a lie in, though not with the knowledge or consent of a parent.
- *Parentally condoned absence*. Described as parents keeping the children away from school. E.g.: parents approved an absence in order to take a child on a family holiday or so that the child could act as a carer.

The SCRE researchers also make reference to the views of other authorities, quoting Stoll (1990) who describes truancy as 'absence from school for no legitimate reason'; Atkinson, Halsey, Wilkin and Kinder (2000) who point out that truancy is a range of behaviours which can take place in circumstances ranging from one lesson to periods of many months; and Kinder, Wakefield and Wilkin (1996) who point out that truants need not even necessarily leave the school premises. As if these different interpretations did not do enough to establish the difficulty of defining truancy, in 2001 Ofsted further stretched the definition by concluding that, since some unauthorized absence results from the school's refusal to authorize excessive absence for holidays during term time, 'truancy is not synonymous with unauthorized absence'. Whilst all of these definitions touch some part of the truth, none can be said to be comprehensive.

The audit commission's figures for absence in England and Wales conclude:

- On any one day 400,000 pupils are absent from school.
- In secondary schools nine million half days are recorded as truancy each year.
- In primary schools five million half days, which can be classified as parentally condoned absence, are lost each year.

In the case of primary schools, SCRE research in 2003 discovered that not only did more primary school pupils truant than was previously thought, but also that a significant number did it without the knowledge of their parents. In one sample, 17 per cent of those claiming to have truanted said they had walked out of school without their absence being detected.

In the light of the British Government's failure to reduce truancy in 2002, it is clear that on a national scale schools and LEAs are faced with a massive problem. If progress is to be made then any new strategies must first recognize the diverse types of truancy, be aware of those pupils who are likely to truant and create responses that more accurately reflect the circumstances of the individual pupil and the individual school.

Condoned truancy (by parents)

This particular type of truancy is amongst the hardest to identify since, with the connivance of their parents, pupils hide the true causes of their absence. Truancy might only be shown to have taken place after painstaking work and investigation by teachers and EWS officers to establish a pattern of absence and discrepancies in the reasons given to justify absence. The difficulty arising in such investigations is that they require, in the first instance, teachers to proceed on the basis of assumptions and to place a question mark over the honesty of a parent or a carer.

Condoned truancy (by teachers)

Faced with large classes and increasing management difficulties in their lessons, there is no doubt that teaching staff feel a degree of relief when some students are absent. This sense of relief is undoubtedly increased when the absent pupils are those members of the class who are usually disruptive. Whilst no one would suggest that teachers are actively encouraging pupils to be absent there can be no doubt that the temptation to be less assiduous in following up absence exists. Given the fact that this temptation exists and accepting the difficulties associated with reintegrating frequently absent pupils, it is understandable that the climate in the classroom might not always be optimum for maximizing attendance and overcoming the effects of absence. It is vital that any school seeking to reduce absence should take note of these factors and offer support and specialist programmes to assist both the teacher and the absentee.

Culturally motivated truancy

In an increasingly multi-ethnic and multi-cultural society, it is inevitable that views about the purpose and value of education will become more diverse. There is no doubt that amongst some cultures the value placed upon education is less than in others. In cultures where there are very strong views about gender roles and there is, for example, an expectation that girls will marry and become 'homemakers and mothers', there is no great value placed upon the intrinsic (and sometimes even the extrinsic) value of education. Staying at home and assisting mother is seen as a better preparation for life. Evidence of this attitude may be apparent at primary level and will be very marked by early adolescence. Similarly, the expectation placed upon boys in some subcultures is that they become a significant part of the economic unit of the family by their early teens. In such circumstances the family gives priority to the child learning the family trade and places little emphasis on formal education.

Economic truancy

The need to contribute to the economic well-being of the family is not restricted to particular ethnic groups in our society. Given the typical profile of most truants, there is often a need and a desire for more money within the family. The notion of deferred gratification promoted by schools does not sit comfortably with families where there is a culture of short-term decision-making, brought about by financial strains, and no history of academic success. If children are encouraged to work rather than to attend school, or alternatively if their parents are obliged to work such long hours that they are frequently absent from the home, the culture of personal organization and school attendance is never firmly established.

The school phobic

There is no doubt that some children develop a phobia associated with attendance at school and, as with any other phobia, genuinely find it difficult to deal with the situation due to the anxiety they experience. Labels like 'school refuser' exacerbate the problem by implying that there is a deliberate desire on the part of the absentee to confront and reject the values of the school. In truth the phobia is an illness like any other and the pupil should be no more liable to judgement than any other child who has a genuine illness that prevents attendance. In such cases the school should consult with the parents and facilitate meetings with the relevant professionals to explore and address the underlying causes of the condition. (See Chapter 4.)

Post-registration truancy

In view of those research findings which indicate that pupils are likely to absent themselves from lessons without actually leaving the school premises, the assumption that the presence of a child at registration twice a day indicates attendance at lessons could well be erroneous. On that basis schools would be well advised to employ methods for checking attendance regularly, throughout the day.

Fear of failure

In a school environment that is increasingly concerned with testing, it is important that parents and teachers are mindful of the pressures faced by pupils. If the expectation to 'perform well' gets out of proportion then it is possible that pupils will react by displaying a total or partial rejection of the school's values. Children at the stage of primary–secondary transfer have been found to be particularly sensitive to the pressures caused by the expectation to do well, and in consequence to have fears about their ability to cope in the new school.

Insecurity/personal safety

There is evidence that personal safety and a sense of well-being play a significant part in a pupil's willingness to identify with the school, and in some cases in their willingness to attend. Surveys of prospective Year 7 pupils and parents regularly indicate that a high priority is placed upon the need to feel that the school provides a safe and caring environment for its pupils. In many cases this consideration is listed as equal in importance to academic success when selecting a school.

Work by the author in Cheshire schools revealed the importance to pupils of feeling safe in the school environment. Though the concern was not restricted to any particular year group, it was viewed by all as particularly significant at the point of transfer from primary to secondary education.

Rejection of values

All acts of truancy, to a greater or lesser extent, involve some rejection of the values promoted by the school. It is this rejection rather than the absence itself that might be said to characterize truancy. In that sense, therefore, it is possible for a pupil to be physically present in school or in a lesson but mentally to be truanting. This 'near truancy' where, despite their presence, pupils are 'switched off' is part of a spectrum of 'routine deviance' that was identified in the Elton Report in 1989. Behaviour patterns in this spectrum that resemble truancy and may be similarly motivated include:

- *Deliberate lateness*: to school or to lessons
- *Switching off*: not paying attention, not offering answers, packing up early, ceasing work, etc.
- *Disruptive behaviour*: 'messing about', not remaining on task, diverting the teacher's attention to slow the pace of a lesson, engineering confrontation in order to be excluded and thereby avoid work
- *TOOT*: talking out of turn
- *HOC:* hindering other children
- *Avoidance tactics*: queuing to have a book marked, frequently breaking off work to sharpen pencils, asking permission to turn a page, frequent visits to the toilet, waiting unnecessarily for the teacher's permission to proceed rather than seeking advice.

4 Where Does Truancy Start?

Early socialization

There are numerous reasons why truancy starts in a child and an equally large number of strategies that might be employed to address the situation. However, one thing that is generally agreed is the frequent cyclical nature of truanting behaviour. Education Welfare Workers often find, when dealing with cases of truancy, that there is a culture of non-attendance within families, and this culture often mirrors the parents' own poor levels of attendance during there own school careers.

'Truancy and School Exclusion', a report prepared by the Social Exclusion Unit in 1998, found that the majority of truants tended to be older pupils and from poorer backgrounds. Parents of truants were less likely to be owner-occupiers, tended to live in local authority housing and usually worked in low-skilled rather than professional jobs. For boys, living in a single parent family appeared to increase the likelihood of truancy, though overall there was no apparent gender bias.

In the 2003 SCRE report it was noted that a larger number of primary school pupils than expected (27 per cent) said they had truanted without the collusion of their parents and 17 per cent of these cases said they had been able to leave school without detection. Additionally, although more boys than girls truanted from primary schools, girls in Years 7, 8 and 9 of all white secondary schools were more likely to truant than boys. In schools of a mixed racial intake more boys than girls truanted in Years 7 and 8. Very few secondary pupils from ethnic minorities admitted to truancy.

Stereotypical background of the truant

- Pattern of social deprivation. Unemployment. Poor housing. Income below the average. Family in receipt of benefit.
- No role model at home. No one with previous educational success. Likely to have a disrupted family structure e.g. single parent, parent in need of care. Parents may be absent for economic reasons/constraints of employment.
- Families might desire success but lack the necessary skills. No firm concept of parenting skills. No knowledge of education process. No skills to access or communicate with school structures.

The 1998 report by the Social Exclusion Unit noted the role of the family in influencing truancy:

'Poor parental supervision and a lack of commitment to education are crucial factors behind truancy ... Some families condone unauthorized absence, for example for family shopping trips. Others expect school-age children to look after younger brothers or sisters during the day, or to take on excessive responsibility for helping out at home.'

In the same report teachers and LEAs regularly cited family circumstances or values as regular causes of non-attendance, and Home Office figures revealed 'a statistical relationship between truancy and strong attachment to siblings or friends in trouble with the police'. Nevertheless the report also concluded that 'The influence of families and peers is matched by the effects of problems at school'.

Ofsted findings quoted in the report revealed that poor attendance in some schools is ' ... centred amongst pupils who are weak readers'. Ofsted also found that anxiety about examinations and bullying were strong influencing factors, and that ' ... dislike of a particular teacher and/or a failure to see the relevance of the National Curriculum were also significant causes of truancy'.

Early school experiences

SCRE research published in 2003 (*Absence from school: A study of its causes and effects in seven LEAs*) found that the reasons for truancy were contested and that different interest groups laid emphasis upon different causes.

- *Pupils* were more likely to blame school-based factors rather than home-related issues. The reasons offered by secondary pupils included bullying, problems with teachers, problems with lessons, feeling isolated and peer pressure. Primary pupils also included bullying in their list of major reasons for truancy as well as boredom, a dislike of teachers and the avoidance of tests.
- *Parents* in the main felt that school-related factors were the cause of truancy. They cited bullying, problems with teachers and the influence of friends as the main factors. Whilst most parents thought that education was valuable, the parents of poor attenders were less positive in their views of school and were more likely to condone absences.
- *LEAs and Teachers* accepted that a range of factors caused truancy but, for the most part, laid emphasis upon home factors such as poor parenting, poor organization and a perception that education was unimportant. Primary teachers took the view that truancy was almost entirely condoned by parents, but secondary teachers said that factors such as inappropriate curriculum, school systems, bullying, racial harassment, inappropriate teaching methods and peer pressure were also important factors. Some secondary school teachers also felt that low self-esteem and embarrassment at perceived inadequacies were significant factors.

The researchers also discovered a very strong view amongst teachers that truancy is cyclical. According to teachers, pupils 'got into the swing of staying off.' It was then increasingly difficult for pupils to return to school and catch up. According to one teacher, truant pupils were 'caught in a vicious circle and hated seeking help.' This 'snowball' phenomenon, say the researchers, thus became an unending pattern of cause and effect. In these circumstances, and in others mentioned below, the need to 'nip behaviour in the bud' is clearly of major importance

Within the same research primary teachers further expressed the view that pupils who were often absent had difficulty in making and keeping friends, whilst pupils felt that the habitual truant displayed a 'funny attitude' towards them. Non-attenders quickly became lost and isolated. When they returned to school they were usually out of touch and behind with both work and play. They did not fit in and this contributed to their unhappiness. One home-school liaison teacher said that '. . . the children who are here all the time play their games . . . the child who has been off does not know how to play the games, does not know who to go to, so they become lonely.'

Teachers also thought that poor attenders lost confidence easily. They became frustrated, bad-tempered, undisciplined and insecure. Absence meant they lost the security of a routine, causing a reduction in performance and with it a loss of self-esteem. This cycle was also noted at secondary level but, by then, was more acutely manifested.

Learned behaviour

Clearly, particularly amongst young children there is such a close link, in every respect, between early socialization and early school experience that it is often impossible to draw a clear line between the two. On this basis it is important that any strategies employed to combat non-attendance involve the parents as much as possible.

Having involved the parents and secured their cooperation to ensure attendance, there will still be problems that the school and the support services will have to address. Securing attendance is only the start of the process. Often, by the time that any meaningful intervention can take place, learned behaviours will be embedded. Given the stereotypical background of the truant, it is likely that children will lack basic social and coping skills. It may well be that they have been unused to encouragement and support. Their self-image might need particular attention, their thinking skills might be below average and they might well be in the habit of giving up when faced with a problem rather than approaching it with imagination or determination. Often reluctant attenders, even though they are in the school environment, will practise avoidance tactics. They will fail to join in discussions or answer questions, they will often 'be stuck' and not make progress with their work. They may need extra reassurance to progress to the next stage or will frequently be found in the queue to sharpen their pencil so that they can put off the next challenge.

Intervention and support

Whilst the background to some problems is likely to be in the home, it will be up to the school to ensure that an integrated policy of intervention is arrived at and carried out. The first challenge will be to ensure that parents realize that the school is trying to help the pupil rather than blame or punish the parents. If non-attendance is dealt with on the basis of threats and punishment at this early stage, there is every likelihood that a barrier will develop between school and home and the young truant will eventually become an older, disruptive pupil who fails to complete their formal education.

Once the parents have been enlisted as willing partners in the process of improving attendance and raising achievement, then the various arms of the Education Welfare Service can combine to give parents the skills and resources to support the child (and indirectly the school) still further. Raising a pupil's self-esteem in this way will inevitably enhance their ability to access the education process. (See information on Parenting Courses in Chapter 2.)

Above all, the SCRE report expressed the view that, irrespective of the complexity of causes,

> 'Truancy starts young. Many pupils begin truanting in primary school and continue to do so in secondary school. Therefore, early intervention would be worthwhile to prevent pupils developing the habit.'

School refusal/school phobia

School refusal, often referred to as school phobia, is a complex emotional condition that accounts for something like five per cent of all child psychiatry referrals. The most obvious manifestation of the condition is the fact that the child experiences great anxiety associated with school and has great difficulty attending. Despite this non-attendance however, school refusal is not truancy and should be approached and treated in a different way.

The term 'school refusal' describes the behaviour of children who experience acute anxiety and an irrational fear of going to school. It is a condition most likely to manifest itself at points of transition in a child's life. It is therefore likely to occur on entry into school at age 5, at the point of transfer to secondary school at age 11 and with the onset of adolescence, between the ages of 14 and 16. About 15 per cent of children are likely to experience some form of school phobia at one point or another in their school life.

SCHOOL REFUSAL	TRUANCY
School refuser stays at home when off school	Truant may stay at home but will not necessarily do so
Child exhibits acute anxiety when preparing to go to school but does not exhibit any anti-social behaviours	Child exhibits other anti-social behaviours in and out of school
Child is often anxious by nature and concerned about conforming	Child does not necessarily exhibit specific anxiety although underachievement may prompt behaviour
No association with class by either income or occupation	Likely to be associated with lower income groups working in manual/unskilled employment
Often family history of neurosis	Often history of low achievement at school. Education not valued
Over-protective parents	Often poor parenting skills and inconsistent discipline
Often absent or ineffective father	Often single parent family (particularly so with boys)
No gender bias	No gender bias

SCHOOL REFUSAL	TRUANCY
Family size not significant though the youngest child is often most vulnerable in a larger family	Family size not particularly relevant though other family members may be 'anti-school' or exhibit anti-social behaviour
Struggles to relate to peers in school due to absences and anxiety when in school	Often very influenced by peers
Often average ability or able and anxious about academic performance	Not committed to school values. May be below average, lower reading age etc.
Peak incidence at ages 5, 11 and 14–16	May occur at any age but peaks at age 14 and 16

Figure 4.1 Comparison between likely features of a truant and a school refuser

Possible triggers for school refusal/school phobia

- Starting school for the first time and fearing separation from the known environment (often mother) of the home.
- Starting a new school (primary/secondary transfer).
- Moving house and starting a new school, making new friends, etc.
- Returning to school after a long illness or after a long holiday.
- Feeling a failure at school or fearing situations which 'expose' the individual, such as tests or reading aloud in class.
- Finding difficulty in making friends or having no friends.
- Feeling isolated or separate from the crowd in some way, being chosen last for teams, feeling embarrassed in the showers.
- Safety issues like being bullied, or fearing the possibility of being bullied.
- Violence or abuse in the home, inflicted on the child or another family member.
- Problems in the home such as rows, separation, divorce and associated uncertainty.
- The illness of someone in the home or a close family member like a grandparent.

- Bereavement: the loss of someone in the home, a close friend, family member or even a pet.
- The loss of attention and the fear of being replaced with the arrival of a new baby.
- Experiencing or witnessing some sort of traumatic event like an assault or a serious accident.
- Experiencing anxiety associated with the journey to school such as agoraphobia, fearing for one's personal safety, feeling uncomfortable on the bus or the train.

Recognizing school refusal/school phobia

Given the diversity of the above list, the reasons for the child's anxiety may not be immediately apparent, and when questioned the child may well find it impossible to identify the source of the anxiety. Since school refusers are not often naughty children the uncharacteristic nature of their behaviour can add to the anxiety and increases the confusion of their parents.

School phobia can develop slowly or it may appear suddenly and dramatically. At first parents are unlikely to identify the condition, since it is often manifested in the form of physical symptoms such as nausea, vomiting and stomach pains. These symptoms are likely to be construed as genuine but will often disappear at the weekend or during the day when the child has become sure that they will not be sent to school.

At one time it was thought that school phobia was caused entirely by a child's fear of separation from its mother and that overprotective parents subconsciously encouraged the situation. However, whilst this may be true in part with younger children, the above list makes it clear that there are wider causes than simply the fear of separation. In many cases a child will prove to be vulnerable in some way. Sometimes a child will be overweight or has suffered a major illness. Alternatively parents might have lost another child at birth or in infancy and have reacted by becoming overprotective.

Managing the return to school

In every case the solution to the problem of school refusal/phobia is for the child to return to school. Failure to manage the return correctly will almost certainly make the situation worse. When a child is allowed to stay at home, the safety of that environment contrasts starkly with the anxiety felt in the school situation. If this is allowed to persist then encouraging a return becomes increasingly difficult. In broad terms, it is preferable for school refusal/phobia to be tackled early since it is generally held that the problem becomes more difficult to treat if it is allowed to persist or if it occurs in later adolescence. The management of the child's return to school is dealt with in Chapters 2 and 9.

Conclusion

When faced with the amount and variety of evidence relating to the causes of truancy it would be easy to think that the problem is too diverse and too complex for the school to tackle. Nevertheless, we have a moral mandate to search for solutions because, regardless of the diversity of opinions, it is the child who is at the centre and it is the child who should be the focus.

Amongst the diverse views reported in 2003 by the SCRE, truants themselves cited problems with lessons, teachers, bullies and friends as the major causes for their truancy and often fell back on the blanket reason of boredom. Experienced teachers however, will be aware that the word boredom is often shorthand for a lack of understanding and, in the context of truancy, may well say a lot about the truant's sense of self and their ability to cope.

Parents, for the most part, offered similar reasons for truancy but, in the majority of cases, did not place a high value on school. In the view of teachers, (particularly primary teachers) parents were usually complicit in the absence and failed to give the right type and amount of support to their children.

LEAs and secondary teachers, on the other hand, were less likely to place so much blame on the parents. Whilst they too cited all of the reasons given above, they also felt that an inappropriate curriculum or low levels of ability left pupils feeling embarrassed by their inability to cope and resulted in low self-esteem.

In the final analysis it is this lack of self-esteem that ties together all the different causes and contributory factors. Pupils who, through home background and/or lack of ability, fail to engage with the school process are, from the very start, plunged into a spiral of failure that, almost inevitably, results in one form of truancy or another. Their inability to relate to others or to cope with the work leaves them feeling isolated and threatened. Their resulting absences leave them further behind, resented by other pupils who see them 'rewarded' with extra attention from the teachers, and resented by the teachers who experience an increase in workload and see the truant as an obstacle to achieving performance targets. Comments from teachers such as '[Absence] drags down their marks . . . I try to help . . . that takes time and the other children are missing out', and from other children such as 'They just waste their . . . education and turn out to be thickos . . . I wouldn't want to be friends with them. There's no point if you don't see them' bear this out and clearly indicate that any move to combat truancy must combat much wider social and emotional issues.

5 What Happens to Truants

With the raising of the school leaving age to 16 in 1973, the idea that all pupils should leave school with some sort of qualifications gained ground and came to be accepted by the vast majority of schools, pupils, parents and employers. However, there continues to be a small number of pupils in every school for whom education, let alone qualifications, is something to avoid rather than embrace. It is towards these students that we must target our efforts, since the outcomes of their non-attendance have significance for us all.

In the past it was possible and relatively easy to get a job without qualifications, and from that job followed:

- Identity
- Role
- Self-esteem
- Means of achieving
- The opportunity to realize aspirations

Today, with the education system so intent upon raising the standard of learning and the levels of qualifications, it is not surprising that employers have become more rigorous in their expectations when advertising for and appointing personnel. Indeed, so inextricably linked are the policies of the British Government and the expectations of employers that it is sometimes difficult to determine which is the 'truck' and which the 'trailer'. What is entirely clear, however, is that in the modern labour market a lack of qualifications means that success is at best unlikely and at worst impossible.

Failure at school does not prevent aspiration

If the desire to realize aspirations remains, despite an absence of the wherewithal to do so, then it follows that individuals will evolve strategies that will allow them to succeed irrespective of the difficulties that they face. In an ideal world it would be very nice to think that once faced with the problem the aspirant would identify the solution and embark upon a course of study to gain the necessary qualifications and subsequent employment. Whilst such a course of action is not without precedent, for the most part solutions to such problems are rarely so straightforward and, given the complexity of issues related to truancy, are never so simple.

The stark truth is that absence from school is a life-changing experience. It removes choice from the absentee, it alienates them from agencies that might offer support and it creates problems that become further barriers to success and a lifestyle that would generally be accepted as conventional. For those pupils who have a history of absence from school there is a significantly higher likelihood that they will become:

- Unemployed
- A teenage parent
- Homeless in later life
- Involved in criminal activity
- Involved in some level of substance abuse
- The subject of a custodial sentence

Current statistics reveal that:

- 23 per cent of school age defendants appearing in court have some history of truancy.
- 50 per cent of all young offenders have been excluded at some point in their school career.

Figures for inner London reveal that:

- 40 per cent of all burglaries
- 50 per cent of all muggings
- 30 per cent of all car thefts

are committed by juveniles (possibly above the school leaving age but still classed as young offenders) who are currently truanting or who had a history of truancy during their school career.

The evidence of these figures leaves little doubt that the costs of truancy go far beyond the truant's failure to gain meaningful qualifications or realize their full potential whilst at school. Such behaviour is often a product of the truant's socialization and unless the cycle is broken the likelihood is that the behaviour will be passed on to future generations.

Any effective initiative to improve attendance must therefore include strategies to re-educate parents as well as offering a curriculum and an environment that will keep pupils in school and offer them the opportunity to succeed.

The views and backgrounds of young offenders

In compiling this section the author visited Her Majesty's Young Offenders' Institution, Thorn Cross, Cheshire to meet with and interview a number of inmates and to hear their experiences first hand. The inmates cooperated readily and showed a genuine interest in the exercise. In all cases their anonymity has been safeguarded but for ease of reference initials have been used to distinguish between responses.

How the research was conducted

The participants in the survey (21 in number) were selected at random from one wing of the young offenders' institution, and had an average age of 19 years and 7 months. The shortest sentence being served was nine months and the longest eight years. Many were serving concurrent sentences for multiple offences. For five this was their first offence, though for one this was his thirty-seventh conviction and his fifth custodial sentence. Each inmate was interviewed in private. All of the participants answered the same questions (see Appendix B) and their responses were recorded at the time of the interview. In all cases the participants offered additional information and this, with some quotes, is included after the tables of results.

Inmate	Truant	Excluded	Truancy detected/ Follow up	Drug/ Alcohol habit	Drug/ Alcohol related crimes	Offences whilst truanting
GP	Yes	Yes from main and special education	Detected. No follow up	Drugs Pre-16	No	D/T/MV/CD
LS	No	No	N/A	Drugs Pre-16	Yes	None
MH	Yes	Failed to attend in Year 11	Detected. No follow up	Drugs Pre-16	Yes	D/T/S
PW	Yes	Yes	Detected. No follow up		Yes	D/T
DF	Attended but was a mental truant	No	Never dealt with by teachers		No	None
AHa	Yes	Yes. No school after Year 9	Detected. No follow up	Drugs Pre-16	Yes	D/T/MV/V
AHb	Yes	No	Undetected		Yes	None
GT	Yes	No	Detected and punished	Drugs Pre-16	Yes	None
AP	Yes	Yes	Detected. No follow up	Drugs Pre-16	No	D/T/V/B

Inmate	Truant	Excluded	Truancy detected/ Follow up	Drug/ Alcohol habit	Drug/ Alcohol related crimes	Offences whilst truanting
ME	Yes	Yes x 2	Detected. No follow up after Year 10	Drugs Pre-16	Yes	D/T
AC	Yes	Yes x 5 for violence, finally to secure special unit	Always detected. Follow up	Drugs Pre-16	Yes	D/T/V
NAa	Yes	No	Undetected		No	None
CK	No	To special education			Yes	S.14 Convictions
BR	Yes	Yes	Detected. No follow up after Year 10	Drugs Pre-16	Yes	D/T/MV/H
PD	Yes	Yes	Detected. No follow up after Year 10	Drugs Pre-16	Yes	T/MV/H
NAb	Yes	Yes	Detected. No follow up after Year 10	Drugs Pre-16	Yes	D/T/MV

Inmate	Truant	Excluded	Truancy detected/ Follow up	Drug/ Alcohol habit	Drug/ Alcohol related crimes	Offences whilst truanting
SD	Yes	No	Detected. No follow up	Drugs Pre-16	Yes	V
PL	No	No	Undetected		Yes	S
KK	Yes	Temporary	Detected and punished	Drugs Pre-16	Yes	D/MV/CD
SK	Yes	Yes	Detected and punished		No	MV/V
JD	Yes	Yes	Detected and punished		No	MV/H/O/S

Figure 5.1 Attendance and offending patterns

KEY CD= Criminal Damage. D= Drugs. H= Handling Stolen Goods. MV= Motor Vehicle. O= Carrying an Offensive Weapon. S= Shoplifting. T= Theft. V= Violence.

Although the sample used for this survey was small it never-theless bears out the existing statistics available and clearly indicates that the failure to offer meaningful education to some members of the school community has far reaching and costly repercussions both for the individual and society at large. In percentage terms the figures for those interviewed (21 in number) were as follows:

	%
Truanted at some point in school career	90.4
Excluded at some point from school	57.1
Excluded or simply ceased attending school	61.9
Had an established drug or alcohol habit whilst at school	66.6
Imprisoned for crimes committed under the influence of drugs or alcohol	71.4
Committed crime whilst truanting (though not always caught and convicted)	78.9
Truanted without being detected or felt that there was no meaningful sanction or follow up on the part schools or the EWS	73.6
Truanted with parental knowledge and/or connivance	26.3
Left school with no formal qualifications	47.6
Left school with advanced qualifications	4.76

Figure 5.2 Percentage breakdown of truancy-related behaviour

From the above table it will be clear that less than half of the respondents gained qualifications from school, and in only one case were those qualifications at an advanced level. A more detailed breakdown of attainment levels revealed the following information:

	%
5 or more GCSE passes at grades A–C	14.2
3 GCSE passes at grades A–C with other passes at grade D or below	14.2
2 GCSE passes at A–C with other passes at Grade D or below	4.76
1 GCSE pass at grade A–C with other passes at grade D or below	9.5
4 GCSE passes or more at grade D or below	4.76

Figure 5.3 Formal qualifications gained by interviewees whilst at school

Employment history

Of those interviewed, only six out of 21 (28.57%) had never had a job. However, of the remainder only five had held permanent jobs. Two had been with the armed forces, one leaving after 22 months due to an accident and the other after 14 months when his mother died. Both had juvenile records and a history of truancy and 'turned to crime' when they couldn't get jobs.

In the opinion of many, a poor school record meant that they had little prospect of a 'good job', and crime was the only way of making a decent living and getting what they wanted from life. For others, the lack of direction and interest in school had become a habit by the age of 16. There was nothing that they were interested in doing and crime both filled their time and brought rewards. Drugs and alcohol played a major part in unemployment. In some cases substance abuse had led to the sack but in others the cost of the habit meant that employment offered insufficient rewards to buy the necessary drugs or alcohol. Crime on the other hand paid well and was therefore pursued 'out of necessity.'

Since the age of 16 only six of the 21 (28.57%) interviewed had undertaken any form of training. Two had completed their basic training with the army, one had learned painting and decorating whilst working for his father shortly before sentencing, and one had followed a day release course in sheet metalworking for three months after leaving school but 'packed it and the job in after three months'. Two of the first offenders, both serving sentences for alcohol-related crimes of violence, had followed more traditional training routes. One had attended sixth form college and gained AS and A-Level qualifications, whilst the other had completed a joinery apprenticeship with the local authority and had passed NVQ Levels One and Two. In neither case was there a history of truancy or disruption whilst at school.

Qualifications gained in prison

In all but two cases the inmates questioned had joined the prison education programme and felt that they had benefited from the type of courses offered. The level of courses had been tailored to suit the needs of the candidates and the range of subjects offered catered for a wide range of interests.

By far the most popular were courses in computing, numeracy and literacy. The level of course offered ranged from the very basic (two prisoners had learned to read and write) through to GCSEs and, in one case, specialist correspondence courses had been sought and obtained for the inmate who was already qualified to A-level.

In addition to academic courses a wide range of vocational courses was offered which included catering, health and fitness subjects, engineering, all of the construction trades and industrial cleaning. Once again the courses were tailored to cater for the needs of the learners and ranged from the very basic to NVQs. Alongside these qualifications the Education and Psychology Departments ran an extensive enrichment programme that included courses such as thinking skills, anger management, first aid and parenting skills.

All of the inmates felt that the prison, in contrast to school, offered them courses that interested them, had some relevance and value, were suited to their ability and gave them the opportunity to succeed. A number of the inmates believed that the small group sizes meant that they felt valued and supported in their learning, whereas in school they felt lost in big groups and could never keep up. This frustration had led many to truant in the first place and their absences had exacerbated the problem and set the spiral of failure in motion.

The success that many of the inmates felt was also closely associated with the length of the courses. This was particularly true of the less able and those who had failed to develop any form of study habits at school. In their view, traditional courses, like

GCSEs, took too long to complete and only the most able had opted to study at that level. The majority felt that the modular nature of entry level and NVQ courses offered more encouragement through regular feedback and the opportunity to gain pass grades as each task was completed. One prisoner summed up the success of the education programme when he remarked that he had 'been able to achieve' and that 'prison had made him feel good about himself'.

Plans after prison

When asked about their plans after prison the majority of those interviewed had clear ideas about what they wanted to achieve. However, experienced staff members in the Prison Education Department were quick to point out that planning for the future was a popular pastime for many inmates. Such plans were rarely based upon a realistic assessment of the problems they were likely to face or the temptations they were likely to encounter when they returned to their home environment. This view was to some extent borne out by one inmate who admitted that apart from working in a bar on a casual basis and once taking a computer course 'to please his mum', he'd never actually had a job. Despite this he confidently declared that on release he would try to get a job as a graphic designer even though he only had five GCSEs, no qualification in art and no relevant experience. Given these circumstances it is not surprising that young offenders, who already feel that the system has failed them, should be easily discouraged upon their release and that the incidence of re-offending remains high.

These considerations notwithstanding, some of those questioned did have very positive plans. Eight of them said that they had been promised jobs, often with family members, whilst five more were quite clear that they wanted to enrol on training courses and continue the learning that they had started in prison. If all were successful then such a number (61.9%) would be a real success story. In any event what was patently clear was that all of those answering positively had been influenced by, and interested in, the courses offered by the prison, in direct contrast to their school experiences. If they could overcome other social and personal challenges it seemed likely that they would be reasonably well placed to change their lifestyles.

Of the remaining eight inmates interviewed, five said that they thought they would get jobs and mentioned employment related to the courses they had followed. Unlike the others, however, they had made no enquiries, had no substance to their plans and when questioned more closely struggled to put flesh upon the bones of the idea. One other interviewee said that maybe he would get a job but that he wasn't really bothered. Of the two remaining inmates, one said he, 'had no plans to work. He had a car and a flat on the outside and would go back to crime [supplying drugs]' but would be 'more careful this time'. The other said that he had 'had trials as a professional footballer but drugs had wrecked that . . . there was no future in a way'. His answer was that he would return home, get a part-time job – 'any job' – so he could 'tell the police where he got his money from' and then he would 'sell [drugs] again to make decent money'.

This same inmate talked with some pride about one brother who had just graduated from Oxford, and another who had passed eight GCSEs and was studying for A-levels.

This contrast in family fortunes seemed to sum up the damage that failure at school and truancy can do to the life and aspirations of an individual. At the same time it left the interviewer with the thought that, regardless of the amount of time and effort invested, education cannot, on some occasions, offer the perfect answer to every problem faced.

On a more optimistic note it did seem that prison had changed the views and aspirations of some of the young offenders. Accepting that to be the case, schools, with the opportunity for earlier intervention, ought to be able to adapt and do the same for some if not all of those pupils who currently reject what is being offered.

Personal comments and observations

GP, age 20: 'Since I was 14 I've spent five years inside. I used to feel frustrated at [primary] school. I couldn't do it so I ran home. When I went back I still couldn't do it and all the other kids laughed at me. At special school they cared but back at secondary was just as bad. I forged notes and had a spliff [smoked cannabis].'

MH, age 19: 'It was OK until we moved in Year 9. I just stopped going, I had no mates.'

PW, age 19: 'When Dad left in Year 8 Mum let me stay off. I got suspended then kicked out ... I didn't go to another school. They put me in a home. I was angry. I wish they'd made me stay at school or do cars or construction.'

AHa, age 21: 'Where I went was racist so I did a lot of fighting. They put me in isolation so I bunked [truanted]. I've done loads of courses to stop boredom ... I've seen people about being a youth worker with kids like I was. I want to do that.'

AP, age 19: 'I might work in construction, if not I'll sell [drugs]. It's not fair I got four years [for aggravated assault and robbery]. They [drug dealers] get two and have cars and homes to go back to.'

ME, age 20: 'We moved a lot so I went to four secondary schools. I was excluded from two and never really went to the last one. I know I was bad but they should have put their foot down. I got four Cs and never went. I think they were just glad to be rid of me.' (ME says he intends to return to crime.)

AC, age 19: 'They should have had anger management at school.'

BR, age 20: 'I was kicked out for six months in Year 7 [for fighting] and again in Year 9. By Year 11 I couldn't do it so I never went.'

PD, age 20: 'I've learned to read and write in prison. They gave me one-to-one [tuition] here and helped me.' (PD was excluded from two schools.)

SD, age 20: 'When I was little we moved. I was frightened and shy. My Dad said I had to stick up for myself. I did and it became a habit. I used to get in trouble for fighting so now and again I would sag it [truant] and smoke weed [cannabis] or drink. I've lost three jobs through drink and landed in here.'

Conclusion

Though some of the above quotes leave room for optimism there is, nevertheless, a strong sense that some of those interviewed are already lost souls. In the case of those taking positive steps to change their lifestyles one must inevitably ask: could something have been done sooner to prevent their truancy and the subsequent human and financial costs? There can never be a straightforward answer to that question but it would seem at the very least that there is much evidence to support the view expressed by the SCRE in their 2003 study for the DfES that '... the case for early intervention is very strong'.

6 What Can We Do?

Improving attendance

Some pupils don't attend school. That is a fact of life and all available statistics would seem to indicate that it is a permanent state of affairs. There is no 'golden bullet' or 'quick fix' that will change this situation, and any strategy to improve attendance will have more in common with painting the Forth Bridge than with miracle cures.

The only things that consistently succeed when schools seek to improve attendance are money and time. This has been shown to be true whenever the British Government or individual schools have allocated specific funding to attendance and is born out by the findings of Ken Reid, author of several well-respected works on the subject of attendance. However, Reid and other researchers have also noted that the schools that get the best results are those with their 'backs against the wall'. These schools need success so they prioritize attendance, motivate their staff and achieve results.

Having accepted the importance of money then this must obviously be a major consideration. However, since funds in every school are limited and the EWS has no extra money to offer, schools must also look to motivation and ask themselves certain questions:

- How important is good attendance?
- Why does the school want to improve attendance?
- Why does it matter?
- Is improved attendance something that the management and *all* of the staff want to achieve?
- Has the policy been thought through?
- Is improved attendance seen as an integral part of enhancing achievement and general school improvement?

The answers to those questions must, in the first place, become embedded in the ethos of the school and, in the second place, form the basis of any attendance policy that the school develops.

Commitment to a policy will, undoubtedly, make a difference, but schools must remember that commitment means just that. Purges are all very well to launch an initiative and to raise awareness but, as schools turn to other priorities, the impact fades and with it the success of the programme.

Schools that succeed best in improving attendance are the schools that either want to or need to. Assuming that a school makes the commitment to improve attendance then those charged with administering the policy must be very clear about the task they are undertaking. It is not sufficient to simply persuade the staff that improved attendance is the 'new target'. They must be made aware that the process is long-term and ongoing.

Furthermore, staff must be made aware of the broader picture. Improved attendance will have a knock-on effect within the school. Behaviour and attendance are closely linked. Improving attendance will inevitably bring with it behaviour problems. There is no point in bringing pupils back into school if the school has no idea what to do with them or how to deal with their problems when they get there. On the other hand a properly constructed policy brings its own safeguards with it. Whilst it is not possible to exclude a child for not attending, it is possible to exclude for reasons of behaviour. Therefore, if you get a child back into school, and all else fails, then it might be possible to go down the route of exclusion and direct the child towards a more appropriate form of education.

Improving attendance, therefore, has to be part of an integrated policy that seeks to achieve school improvement and that is supported by a strong code of conduct. With the law as it stands pupils, whether they attend or not, remain on the school roll. In an interview with the author, Jonathan Potter, Principal Education Welfare Officer for Warrington in the north-west of England, made the point clearly when he said:

'Schools cannot simply lose children. In or out they are on the roll and count against results. IN, you might improve them.

You'll certainly improve attendance figures. OUT, you lose on both counts.'

Recent research evidence

In their 2003 report the SCRE (Scottish Council for Research in Education) found that current methods for recording absence, particularly for distinguishing between authorized and unauthorized absence, were 'unhelpful'. Schools, they found, applied the terms in different ways. Almost all authorized ten days of absence for 'extended leave' and a large number made it clear that LEA advice was 'open to interpretation and stressed the need for 'flexibility'. The researchers concluded that the classification of absence masks the problem in many schools and focuses teachers on 'ways of presenting statistics' rather than on seeking solutions to the attendance problem'.

In the same report LEAs noted the problems associated with the recording and authorization of absence. In two authorities it was felt that schools felt under pressure to keep unauthorized levels of absence low. The consequence of this, noted by other LEAs, is that when schools authorize absence too readily it makes it more difficult for the EWS to intervene or to bring successful prosecutions against parents or guardians. In extreme cases this inability to intervene may well mean that child protection cases or pupils requiring medical intervention were going unnoticed. One head of social inclusion captured the views of the majority of the LEA's in the survey when she said:

'This distinguishing between the types of reasons for absence encourages us to concentrate on the wrong aspects. [Teachers say] "I want to get a note from your Mum" – but I'm not interested in notes, I want kids in school!'

The management of absence

One of the main problems then in managing absence is defining exactly what we should be dealing with and at what point we should intervene. The SCRE research revealed that the majority of secondary schools gave attendance a high priority, but that primary schools tended to vary in their approach and the need for early intervention was not as widely appreciated.

In general terms the research found that the majority of schools concentrated on five areas when seeking to improve attendance:

- Group awards
- Individual awards
- Improvements to the school ethos and facilities
- Developing primary/secondary liaison
- Creating good relationships with parents

Though the exact nature of these initiatives might have changed from school to school, the researchers found that success was increased where dedicated staff were used to support attendance.

Providing exact statistical evidence that any of these measures actually improved attendance, however, proved difficult. Though all of the strategies were thought to be effective, opinions on the effectiveness of each of them were divided, perhaps suggesting that the profile of individual schools will determine the level of effectiveness of any particular strategy. Many staff appreciated the support and input of the EWS (Education Welfare Officer) but felt that schools would benefit if EWOs had more time to offer.

Whilst noting the mixed opinions of teachers, the researchers nevertheless concluded in their summary that schools need to change:

> 'Many persistent truants reported that they were bored with school. In addition they were more easily able to truant when taught by supply teachers. A stronger focus on retaining staff, developing appropriate teaching styles and school ethos is needed.'

Recording the severity of absence

When schools decide to prioritize attendance they must seek to establish a benchmark for the school and to establish what the normal attendance pattern is. The first step in this process is to ask two fundamental questions:

- Is attendance low because a few children are never here?

or

- Is attendance low because every child has a day off each week or two?

The answers to these questions require an entirely different response. Answering yes to the first has legal implications and will require action from the EWS. Answering yes to the second means that the whole school has to change and staff have to examine what it is that motivates the children to absent themselves in one way or another.

The nature and pattern of absence is something that human resources systems in industry and local government have already examined. The questions facing them are broadly similar. That is to say: how do you measure the impact of absence, and what difference does the frequency of absence make to its severity?

In making this assessment human resources departments often use a standard formula, which is the number of days absent multiplied by the number of occasions. Thus one three-week block of absence (e.g. for a broken wrist) would be expressed as:

15 days × 1 = 15

On the other hand, 15 days absence, over a period of 15 weeks would be expressed as:

15 days × 15 = 225

Results expressed in this manner show a stark difference in the severity of the absence and have revealed in industry that the odd day's absence regularly is far more significant in terms of productivity and efficiency than a block of absence. Blocks of absence are usually known about and can be predicted, or alternatively a likely ending can be fixed so the absence can be catered for. In school and in industry the regular attender who needs to take a block of absence is likely to have done the work/ study effectively up to the point of absence and is likely to continue to do so on their return. Often, in the school situation, such an absentee is likely to seek work and carry out some tasks even though unable to attend. The irregular attender usually has a poor foundation and an unpredictable future, therefore problems escalate and learning/work become disjointed.

Electronic registration
As a method of providing a clear and accurate record of attendance more and more schools are turning to electronic

registration. Often, because these systems record figures so accurately, schools often experience a one or two per cent reduction in attendance when the system is installed. Where the old paper system allowed for judgement or reflection the electronic system must be done there and then and according to a strict set of codes. In the past schools tended to record attendance to the advantage of themselves or the pupils. Now the system is black and white and there is no room for flexibility: the pupil is either in or out.

On the down side there are those teachers who say that the electronic system hides as much as it reveals. They point out, quite rightly, that the paper system presented a pattern on the page and the lines and circles gave clear indication of a child's attendance. If there was a problem then adjacent to the evidence of the problem was the child's address and contact number. When using electronic registration systems, in many schools all the teacher has to do is press a button. There is no feedback, the printout goes to someone else and the form tutor, as first point of contact, is lost.

Clearly then, whilst an electronic system has strengths these only become an asset if the school has an administration system that compiles the data then retrieves it, analyses it and passes it back to staff so that action can be taken. This prerequisite for attendance monitoring was affected in some schools by the 2003 funding crisis and, despite the installation of an electronic system, schools were unable to finance an effective monitoring system. Since that point changes to the school workforce have brought more support staff and classroom assistants into school. Attendance monitoring is one of 24 tasks no longer deemed the responsibility of the teacher. In schools where, quite feasibly, the teachers might nowadays be in the minority, senior staff should be monitoring attendance through the use of education support staff. Where this is not the case then the management must look carefully at its chosen priorities and make urgent alterations to secure an improvement in attendance.

First day contact

Once a school has taken on board changes to its workforce and reviewed the responsibilities of various staff members, it will then become possible to introduce processes that will effectively monitor attendance and identify individual patterns of absence.

First day contact is the most obvious and direct method of intervention that a school can introduce. Its effects are not necessarily instant and for a change to be recorded the system must be permanently and consistently applied. It may take eighteen months or more for the message to get through but, during that period and subsequently, as the cohorts change, pupils and their parents will come to realize that attendance is a major priority within the school. Whilst this strategy might not affect the recidivist truant it will, without doubt, reduce the tendency towards spontaneous and casual absence.

British Government advice

In 2001 the British Government published the booklet 'Together We Can Tackle It', a checklist for police and schools working together to tackle crime and disorder. Schools, the police and other community agencies were offered advice on a number of topics:

Schools should
- Make a firm public commitment to addressing anti-social behaviour so that pupils and people in the locality know that truancy and related anti-social behaviour is taken seriously.
- Identify pupils at risk of involvement in truancy/crime and adopt a multi-agency approach, engaging with pupils, parents, the police, the EWS, the YOS (Youth Offending Service) and other local agencies to address the problem.
- Adopt a whole school approach and involve pupils, parents, teachers and governors in the management of the school, thereby conferring ownership of policies and achievements.
- Introduce the use of an electronic registration system.

The police should
- Carry out truancy sweeps.
- Develop a close relationship with schools to raise awareness of truancy and anti-social behaviour and encourage the reporting of crime.

- Develop youth participation in community projects.
- Develop joint truancy protocols with schools.

Restorative justice

As part of the same programme, restorative justice has been successfully employed in Nottinghamshire and in the Thames Valley. If the system is present at every stage of the school discipline process then more serious breaches of discipline are avoided. The process is ideally suited to the reintegration of students who have been excluded and has been successfully used to deal with persistent truancy and bullying.

The DfES website

This contains a vast amount of material related to truancy and attendance in schools. The information is regularly updated and examines the links between attendance, behaviour, achievement, family circumstance and various other related factors.

Of particular interest to schools is a downloadable resource entitled 'Ensuring Regular School Attendance-Toolkit'. The resource contains a lot of useful material including a Powerpoint presentation, and a range of articles dealing with legislation, model policies, training materials, self-evaluation documents, multi-agency information, expert advice and various case studies from the DfES and a number of LEAs from across England and Wales. The package can be found by carrying out a behaviour and attendance search on the website: www.dfes.gov.uk.

Behaviour Improvement Project (BIP)

BIP is designed to improve behaviour in schools, to reduce truancy, minimize exclusion and ensure that whether excluded or not pupils are engaged in full-time, relevant, supervized activities at all times. This scheme advocates early intervention in behaviour issues to prevent escalation to truancy, exclusion and beyond. Extensive information relating to regulations, legislation and funding can be found on the DfES website.

Behaviour and Education Support Teams (BESTs)

BESTs are another strand of the BIP programme. They are multi-agency teams consisting of professionals from education, health and social care. Their remit is to work with young people between the ages of 5 and 18 who are at risk of developing emotional and behavioural problems that may lead to truancy, exclusion and/or criminal activity. The teams work closely with the young people, their schools and their families to address and change the emotional and behavioural traits that may obstruct or prevent educational success and lead to anti-social behaviour.

The wider and long-term benefits of BIP are set out in the DfES document: *Education and Skills: The Economic Benefits* (available through the DfES website). In the section 'The Value of Education and Skills', the link between poor qualifications, truancy and crime is clearly shown and reference is made to US studies that establish links between quality pre-school education, high school graduation, and the reduction of criminal activity.

Examples of good practice

The following three examples are taken from the DfES booklet 'Together We Can Tackle It'.

Example
One Kent headteacher identified the need to create community links in order to address truancy and exclusions. At-risk pupils were offered work placements (to link earnings with educational achievement) or took part in outdoor pursuit programmes (linking education with enjoyment). A reduction in damage at the school from £100,000 per annum to nothing and a reduction in truancy and exclusion to almost nil demonstrated the success of the project. The programme was allowed to continue and an inspection five years on revealed that most of the gains were still in place.

Example
In the Thames Valley a partnership has been set up between school, police and educational social workers to ensure that pupils are visited at home after two days of unexplained absence. Any issues emerging are addressed.

Example
Using a grant from the Home Office Crime Reduction Programme, Nottinghamshire Police and the LEA have set up a

restorative justice programme. Schools officers have been trained as facilitators whilst school staff and pupils have been trained in the delivery of restorative conferencing and peer mentoring respectively. The system has been used to resolve thefts, bullying and other offences. The success of the programme has brought about a reduction in truancy and exclusions, and pupils dealt with through the scheme have been led to appreciate the consequences of their actions. One youth who harmed two classmates went through the programme and completed his education without being in any further trouble either with the school or the police.

Close to Home project, Milton Keynes

'Close to Home' is a multi-agency early intervention programme established via consultation with various statutory and voluntary organizations. The establishment of the project in 1999 came from the realization that a significant number of young people were missing school and being excluded. The intention therefore was to work with the young people and through early intervention address the problems and reduce the numbers requiring the support of front-line services such as the children's services. Improving attendance and reducing exclusions remain key targets of the project. Currently the project operates within four secondary schools, several middle schools, various local communities and in partnership with a number of local neighbourhood agencies.

In essence the project works with and supports young people at risk of exclusion through the operation of a number of projects in schools and the community. The services offered include:

- Development of community-based activities.
- Development of a varied educational and social programme.
- Development of advice and support structures for the community.
- Individual support for young people on issues such as anger management, motivation and self-esteem.
- Development of group sessions on issues including drug and alcohol misuse.

- Providing training and support for the peer mediation group.
- A pupil drop-in session, held at lunchtimes at a local youth centre.

The project is staffed by three social workers (one of whom is the project coordinator), an anti-bullying worker, a community worker, two youth workers and a part-time project worker.

Further information about the structure, funding and success of this project can be obtained from:

Michael Greenfield, Close to Home Coordinator
Milton Keynes Council, Saxon Court
502 Avebury Boulevard
Milton Keynes
E-mail: closetohome@milton-keynes.gov.uk

A Bit of a Laugh, Bromsgrove Community Awareness Project

This multi-faceted project, originated by Worcestershire and Herefordshire Youth Offending Service and supported by the local Community Safety Partnership, was intended to raise awareness and reduce juvenile crime while at the same time reassuring the local community and developing the self-esteem of the participants.

The project centred upon the performance of the play *A Bit of a Laugh*, written by Ian McCormack and which dealt with juvenile crime issues, specifically aspects of anti-social behaviour involving violence, alcohol, car crime and domestic burglary. The play was, performed by local high school pupils to audiences of Year 7 and 8 pupils, and was first staged in local middle schools. Subsequent performances took place, at the high school, for local politicians, parents and community groups. The pupils chosen to perform the play were not necessarily drama students but were chosen instead on the basis of their educational needs. The first strand of the project, therefore, was intended to improve the confidence of the participants and to develop their identification with school and the education process.

The performances in middle schools were, in essence, peer mentoring programmes which raised audience awareness and allowed teachers and community police officers to follow up the issues with the help of a previously prepared workshop pack. The performances at the high school created links with the performers' parents, reassured the local community and further developed the performers' identity with the school process. All participants viewed the project as a success in that it proved to be a cost-effective method of raising awareness. Additionally it allowed schools, police, YOS and other members of the Community Safety Partnership the opportunity to communicate directly in an effective, non-confrontational way with a variety of groups they wished to target.

The Warrington Wolves Attendance Project

This programme formed part of the British Government's 'Playing For Success' programme, was jointly funded and supported by the European Social Fund, Warrington Borough Council, Connexions and Warrington Super League Wolves, and took place in the education suite at Warrington Rugby League Football Club. The main aim of the project was to assist young people who, for a variety of reasons, during Year 10 of their school career had experienced difficulties with attendance. The intended outcome of the scheme was that the young people would enhance their sense of self and, by maintaining an association with school, develop positive plans for the future. Within one term of joining the scheme 63 per cent of the participants had improved their attendance. The remaining 37 per cent did not improve attendance but nevertheless remained in regular contact with their schools and with the project. All participants pursued an ASDAN (Awards Scheme and Accreditation Network) Bronze award and developed their skills in planning and target setting.

Without exception, schools felt that the project provided tangible benefits for the participants and commented on positive changes such as:

- Improved behaviour
- Improved self-esteem
- A more positive view of school, self and the future

Final attendance figures and outcomes

By the end of the project 70 per cent of participants were still in regular attendance at school and at Warrington Wolves. This figure exceeds normal expectations for those who experience attendance problems in Year 10. A follow-up by Connexions revealed that of the original participants:

- 40 per cent had gained employment
- 40 per cent had enrolled on college courses
- 10 per cent were actively seeking work

No figures were available for the remaining 10 per cent.

Although European funding for this project has since been withdrawn, the Rugby League Club continue to offer courses through the 'Playing for Success' scheme. Under this scheme out-of-hours curriculum support courses are offered to pupils in KS2 and 3. The courses are Key-Skills based and cover numeracy, literacy and IT. Each course lasts for ten weeks and is delivered by specialist teachers, supported by professional rugby players who act as role models and learning mentors. Participating pupils are presented with achievement awards at ceremonies which take place at the stadium and in their schools.

Warrington Wolves' education support programmes have been so successful that for the last four years they have won the award for the best community programme in the Tetley Super League and most recently were awarded the National Sports Industry's award for best Sport in the Community Programme. A grant from the north-west regional development council means that from 2005, in their new stadium, the club will be offering even more education support programmes including providing a base for home tuition courses for reluctant readers, and further attendance related support courses.

Alsop High School Technology College, Liverpool

Alsop High School, Liverpool, is a twelve-form entry 11–19 comprehensive in Liverpool, catering for 1200 pupils. In 2002 the school was enlarged to accommodate pupils from another local comprehensive which was closed down. The attendance percentage at the school which closed was in the lower 80s and although the enlargement of Alsop has brought an injection of cash into the school it has, nevertheless, brought with it pressures that the newly enlarged school has had to address.

Problems facing Alsop High School

- Large and rapid expansion.
- Integration of staff from two schools and induction of new staff.
- Numerous temporary classrooms.
- The effects of an extensive rebuilding and refurbishment programme.
- Integration of pupils from two schools.
- The creation of a single ethos including aspects such as discipline, rewards, sanctions, and attendance.
- Liaison with parents, pupils and the local community.

Christine Eccles, a science teacher at Alsop with extensive experience in dealing with attendance, was appointed Attendance Officer for the enlarged school. She says: 'We knew that we might face problems with attendance and to some extent that happened.' The attendance at the new school fell to 88 per cent and Ofsted, who visited the school in the autumn term, commented upon the situation in their report. 'We had already realized that we would have to go backwards to go forwards' says Christine, 'and although Ofsted recognized the changes we were making they nevertheless pointed out that our attendance should be higher.'

New mixed with old

Alsop High School has placed a high priority on attendance for some time. Since the 1980s they have operated a first day response system, and ten years ago the school piloted the use of the SIMS (School Information Management System) OMR (Optical Mark Reader) registration system in the city. Attendance monitoring was further strengthened by the appointment of attendance tutors, one for KS3 and another for KS4, in 1998. Building on that good practice Alsop has extended the use of attendance tutors and there is now one in each year group working alongside the head of year.

This team is coordinated by Christine, and a deputy head oversees the whole system.

Electronic registration

From September 2004 the whole school transferred to an electronic registration system, which was first piloted with Year 8. The system chosen was CMIS, supplied by MGL. In explaining the choice, Christine refers to Alsop's status as a specialist technology college:

> 'After discussing the options it was felt that the CMIS system would fit best with the existing computer networks in the school and would allow the transfer of all records and reports in the school to a computerized system. Ultimately all staff will be able to operate registration, reporting, recording and all other associated systems through their laptops and the ability to track each pupil accurately will be greatly enhanced.'

Staff reaction

Staff have reacted positively to the new system and anticipate a reduction in their workload. One particularly positive aspect they have noted is that the CMIS on screen display gives a full overview of attendance and performance in the way that 'the old-fashioned paper-based system' did, with the additional benefit of offering information on academic progress and general behaviour.

Pupil reaction

For their part pupils have already noticed differences and have commented to staff. They are aware of the keener tracking systems that are in place, but because the school has emphasized the welfare and achievement benefits of the system it has been received very positively.

General strategies for improvement

The school has retained and strengthened its existing links with parents and has invested a lot of time in communicating the new attendance policy to all involved. First day response has been retained but the new electronic system allows this to be targeted much more effectively. Similarly, the school has, for some time, compiled 'matched' attendance figures to establish if pupils share similar patterns of absence. This process has always been effective, but once again the new system will allow it to be better targeted.

The 'invisible register'

Within the new electronic system the school has been able to develop an 'invisible register' whereby information relating to particular subgroups in the school can be isolated in order to identify trends. Although these figures cannot be separated when attendance returns are submitted to the DfES the process has nevertheless been useful in detecting underlying trends or identifying chronic non-attenders.

These 'invisible' figures are also useful when attendance awards are decided. By isolating the effects of chronic non-attenders on a class's figures it is possible to make allowances and the efforts of the majority can still be rewarded.

Rewards

Attendance assemblies are held every half term and pupils receive prizes in various categories. All pupils with above 90 per cent attendance receive an award of some sort, whilst those with 100 per cent attendance are entered in a raffle for prizes like DVDs or personal stereos.

All prizes are awarded at the discretion of the attendance tutor who considers issues such as effort, illness and data from the invisible register. The school is keen to avoid giving prizes like chocolate that would fly in the face of the healthy school initiative. Instead prizes like early entry into lunch, music CDs or school equipment are awarded. Currently the school is negotiating with local shops and businesses to develop a discount card that good attenders will be able to use at a variety of retail and leisure outlets.

Internal truancy

Although the focus of Ofsted comments was on authorized and unauthorized absence figures, Christine Eccles feels that the use of the electronic register will reduce internal truancy, a problem she believes could increase as the school continues to grow. As part of the initiative in this area the school has invested part of its supply teacher budget in the permanent employment of staff to cover colleague absences. Ralph Crawford, one of the teachers employed in that capacity, commented:

'Our role has real implications for attendance in a school of this size. As permanent members of staff there is an opportunity for us to build a relationship with the children. Supply teachers don't get to know the children so pupils take the opportunity to mislead them and spontaneous truancy can occur.'

Expected outcomes
The target set for attendance in the enlarged Alsop High is 92 per cent and Christine Eccles expects to see a marked improvement by December 2004, though she accepts that her role will be ongoing. 'The important thing', she says, 'is to keep the pupils informed. Often children don't realize how the odd day off mounts up.' Pupils are now given their attendance figures each half term, their form attendance is published on the attendance notice boards and the position is discussed with the form tutor or the attendance tutor. By involving the children in the process teachers have seen real evidence that pupils can take responsibility for their attendance and that they can self regulate. Figures for the 2004 summer term revealed that over ten per cent of Year 11 pupils had achieved 100 per cent attendance in their final year. By contrast, figures for that same summer period indicate that two per cent of the absences in the rest of the school are accounted for by family holidays in term time. 'That', says Christine, 'is the next area we must work on, by educating parents and improving still further our home school links.'

Conclusion

Ultimately to make an impact on attendance, resources are critical. Whether those resources come in the form of direct finance or in the form of time and commitment, there can be no substitute. However, when money and time are tight schools have to prioritize. When a school and a headteacher are judged there are ultimately three main areas of concern:

- The quality of teaching

- The quality of examination results
- Attendance

If attendance is 'acceptable' (and it is in the majority of schools around the country), then priority is given to the other areas. This decision is made easier when schools and teachers realize that the pupils who are brought back into school by attendance initiatives are often:

- The least motivated
- The most disruptive (to the teaching and learning of others)
- The most likely to bring down the examination percentages (by the combined effect of the other two points)

From the British Government's point of view, attendance continues to present problems. Despite a great deal of effort and publicity the levels of unauthorized absence in schools have remained unchanged since official figures were recorded, and targets for reduction have proved to be elusive.

That said, however, there is perhaps some room for optimism. Whilst recorded absence has not fallen, neither has it risen. Given the increased use of electronic registration systems and the more accurate figures that they provide, a lack of change in the attendance figures may well indicate a net improvement.

Whether this net improvement exists or not, what does seem clear is that schools and LEAs must continue to work and to change attitudes. There is still a degree of snobbery associated with learning in Great Britain that engenders pejorative terms like 'swot' and 'bookworm'. It may well be that a balance will only be achieved when the vocational route to qualification is elevated (as in, for example, Germany) to the same level as the academic route.

It is this type of change in perspective that will ultimately make the difference. 'Whipping in' children does not work. They have to be drawn in to our schools. Certainly there has to be a consequence for not attending school: it is, after all a statutory obligation, but the more creative and effective approach might be to ensure that there should be an even more significant consequence *for attending*. This positive consequence must start by putting the child at the centre. Many teachers still take the view that children come to school to be taught. It is their 'job' to turn up and take what is given. It would perhaps be more beneficial to view pupils as consumers and to examine the way the 'product' is presented.

All too often we expect children to turn up and be taught in buildings with inadequate toilets, with poor shelter from the weather during breaks and in a general environment that offers little or no guarantee for the safety of property or of the individual. On this basis the miracle is that so many pupils turn up in the first place. The fact that they do is perhaps not so much a comment on the quality of education that we offer but a symbol of our society's willingness to be lawful, to be governed and to be educated. On this basis the potential to improve attendance is clearly there and we owe it to our children to give them the best possible product in return for their attendance. In consequence, not only will the performance of the majority improve, but fewer will opt out.

Deference to a teacher's status disappeared long ago. The status of a teacher no longer comes to those who demand respect because of their position. It comes instead to those teachers who give their pupils something of relevance in a manner that the pupils value and enjoy. It is this approach rather than compulsion that is most likely to succeed in the end.

7 School-based Factors

Setting out strategies

The causes of truancy are numerous, complex and disputed. Research has shown that, in seeking to explain absence, parents, teachers, pupils and LEAs all offer a subjective view. Inevitably this causes tensions in the search for remedies and creates some disagreement about which strategy will be most effective. Often the only area of consensus is the issue of complexity, and it is from this point that schools should begin to construct their policies for improving attendance.

No single strategy will be effective. Results will be hard to achieve and progress will be hard to measure. Policies will have to be constructed for the long term and the process will be time-consuming. Nevertheless, that investment of time will be worth it. Although solutions are expensive in terms of time, re-admission processes, the cost of tracking and counselling truants is even more expensive. A solution has to be found, since failure is paid for not only by the individual but also by society in general. Schools have no alternative other than to construct an imaginative and mixed programme of policies with the intention of making education a safer, more humane and relevant experience than it currently is for many pupils.

The school day

On the face of it the length of the school day should be a powerful weapon in the fight against poor attendance. The commitment is minimal, leaving much of the day available for other things. It is only ever for five days a week and is punctuated by regular holidays. As a sales package it would seem to be very tempting but the factors that make it so tempting are, in fact a double-edged sword.

The average school week of 25 hours, when multiplied by the 39 weeks of the school year, amounts to just 975 hours in the classroom. In a normal year the total number of hours available is:

365 days × 24 hours per day = 8760 hours

Thus, as a percentage:

$$\frac{975}{8760} \times \frac{100}{1}$$

Time in school amounts to only 11.13 per cent of a child's life. Even when we allow an extra hour per day to acknowledge the possible influence of other factors such as clubs, assemblies, chats with teachers or counsellors, etc., the time still only amounts to 13.3 per cent.

Clearly for the majority of time in their lives children are exposed to influences other than school. Since we, as educators, can have no direct control over those influences we must ensure instead that, at the times when we do have influence, our message is clear, consistent and appealing both for the pupils in our care and for their parents.

Focusing initiatives

In their 2003 report for the DfES, 'Absence from School: A study of its causes and effects in seven LEAs', the Scottish Council for Research in Education (SCRE) found that truancy starts young and becomes a habit. They further found that absence from school affected performance in Key Stage tests. Not only did this reflect badly upon a school's standing in the performance tables, but it also set into motion a cycle of failure in younger children that might lead to loss of self-esteem and further truancy in later years.

In the view of the SCRE the case for early intervention is strong. However, in practice, primary schools tend to concentrate less on attendance strategies than their secondary counterparts, and the majority of funding is directed at attendance initiatives in Years 10 and 11, since that is when the 'bigger' problems of behaviour, crime and unemployment are more apparent.

In the light of this it would seem logical to suggest that we ignore the final years of school, when the die is cast, and concentrate instead on the primary school. If early learning and attendance habits were established at that level, with support offered to families and self-esteem raised amongst pupils, then ultimately the problems of Years 10 and 11 would disappear. Unfortunately, any re-direction of funding would be likely to affect a school's performance in terms of attendance and academic achievement. Since this would be likely to affect league table positions, any such changes would, inevitably, attract fierce resistance.

The simple truth is that it is easier to attract funding for initiatives in Years 10 and 11 when outcomes in terms of progress to employment, juvenile crime, examination results, etc. are more readily measured. Work in primary schools is at a disadvantage because it is too far removed from the outcome. Despite all of the positive and imaginative work in primary school that develops a pupil's enjoyment of learning and raises their self-esteem, it is impossible to prove a connection between that and continued attendance in Year 9.

What has to happen is that schools across the Key Stages must take a more creative view of attendance and jointly take the view that their work is of equal value and should be complementary. Since, by and large, truants can be shown to be of a particular type and are likely to display particular traits, then there should be a combined effort to remove those factors at an early stage. If this can be achieved then, in theory at least, less truancy should occur and that which does occur will be due to a narrower range of causative factors than might otherwise be the case.

Managing transfer

The most obvious way for primary and secondary schools to cooperate is through the management of transfer between the primary and secondary sectors at age eleven. Whilst many of the same principles apply to transfer at any stage, there are some particular concerns associated with the transfer from one school to another:

- Pupils and parents worry about the new school and the differences they might encounter.
- Concern about the size and environment of the new school.
- Worries about the more 'robust' behaviour of older pupils (often fuelled by urban myths about initiation rituals for Year 7 pupils).
- Concern about the need to change rooms and be taught by several teachers.
- The relatively high number of female teachers in the primary sector might make the prospect of male teachers daunting.
- Anxiety about different teaching and learning styles.
- Concerns about 'new subjects' not covered in the KS2 curriculum.
- The apparent decline in achievement experienced by some pupils in Year 7.

Despite the problems of time and resources there can be no doubt that the effort put into a transfer programme will bring its rewards. Apart from allowing pupils to more readily adapt their learning and to feel safe and at ease in their new environment, increased contact between primary and secondary staff improves learning by extending shared professional knowledge.

There is no standard formula for creating an effective transfer programme, since circumstances will vary from one area to another. Quite apart from socio-economic variations in catchment areas, there will also be geographical considerations. Whilst some schools are fed equally by only three or four local primary schools, others might draw their intake in varying numbers from several schools spread across a large area. Although it is impossible to create one policy to cover the needs of every school there are nevertheless certain aspects that must be included and issues to be borne in mind if a transfer programme is to succeed:

- Create transfer programmes by developing on-going and professional relationships between the management and teachers of participating schools.
- Transfer is not just about passing on and receiving records.
- Where possible any programme should follow the LEA's guidelines and protocols. Transfer systems should not be

used as a method of poaching pupils. No system will work if one party suspects that another has ulterior motives.

- Agree a transfer policy that fits the needs of all participating schools.
- Ensure the transfer process includes a mutual understanding of processes such as record keeping, management responsibilities, pastoral care systems, and parental liaison systems. Where possible try to achieve continuity in these processes.
- Ensure that there is a process for highlighting particular issues when pupils transfer. Such issues might include children at risk, family illness, attendance concerns, cared-for children, and the full spectrum of special educational needs.
- Ensure that relevant cultural issues or EAL (English as an Additional Language) issues are highlighted
- Try to ensure a continuity of curriculum and learning styles.
- Secondary phase teachers should seek the advice of primary colleagues when creating new form groups.
- Devise ways of involving parents and pupils in the process.
- Agree and keep to deadlines.
- Include transfer deadlines in the annual calendar of each participating school.
- Ensure that no school feels that they carry an undue burden in the process and bear in mind that secondary schools usually have more flexibility in terms of time and budget than their primary counterparts.

In addition to these points some attempt should be made to have shared inset between the schools and to devise ways in which teachers can visit their counterpart's establishments. These opportunities might come through teaching or observation but could also come through visits to parents' evenings, open days and other similar events.

Many schools that operate successful primary secondary liaison schemes organize events such as primary–secondary art exhibitions, science days and joint sports events. In other schools older pupils taking practical examinations in subjects such as drama or sports science involve Year 6 pupils in their practical examinations, either by coaching them or by involving them in some aspect of a performance. Other performance opportunities come through joint concerts and reciprocal visits to school plays. Such events not only give pupils the opportunity to become familiar with the secondary school environment, but allow parents and younger siblings the same opportunity when they visit as audience members.

The involvement of parents is a key factor in any primary–secondary transfer strategy. Many secondary schools now have sophisticated technology systems and are able to supply their feeder primaries with DVD material that can be shown at primary open days and parents' evenings. By the time that many parents are directly involved in the transfer process they are already familiar with the secondary school and many of its facilities.

When the process of transfer finally begins parents and their children should be supplied with an induction booklet, developed by the participating schools to an agreed format. Booklets should contain information relating to issues such as travel arrangements, the code of conduct, uniform, discipline, pupil safety, etc. Meetings to convey this information should be held both in the primary school and in the secondary school. On at least one occasion the meeting should take the form of an open forum giving parents and pupils the opportunity to ask questions, make observations and feel part of the process. Within the transfer system arrangements should be made to ensure that contact is made with those families unable or unwilling to take an active part in the process and every effort should be made to involve them. Although the development of a formal transfer process takes a lot of time and effort, once embedded it becomes part of the life of all of the schools and is easier to run. Regular meetings to update the process cement the relationships and ensure positive continuity.

The general consensus amongst pupils, parents and schools is that transfer systems remove much of the anxiety associated with change and result in improved learning, better behaviour and increased cooperation. Although it may seem on the surface that the secondary schools are the main beneficiaries, in truth it is the pupils who benefit most. Furthermore the lessons learned from the primary–secondary process enhance transfer at every other stage of the education process and thus improve relationships and attainment for all pupils.

A sense of security

Having managed the transfer of children into a school or through a particular stage of education, there remains much to be done. As we all know from our own social lives there is no point in being invited somewhere, being given the directions, and being told we will be welcome when we get there if, upon our arrival, we find the experience difficult, threatening or generally unwelcoming.

In previous research conducted by the author in Cheshire secondary schools, issues of personal safety and the security of personal property were regularly cited as prime concerns amongst pupils. Indeed, in the view of most pupils in Year 9 or below, these issues were thought to be more important than liking subjects, liking teachers or school rules. The work of the SCRE (referred to elsewhere in this book) found similar concerns, particularly amongst primary school children. In securing an improvement in attendance, therefore, we must be able to offer guarantees about the environment in which we ask children to conduct their learning.

Bullying

In choosing bullying and personal safety matters as issues of major importance in their school lives, pupils interviewed by the author were unequivocal in their view that they were a cause of truancy. Examples cited predictably included violence and name calling, but less predictable were issues such as crowded corridors 'full of bigger children' and having somewhere to keep your own things safe. There was general agreement that these issues were sufficient to lead to truancy or at least contemplating truancy. Lunchtimes were cited as the 'most dangerous times' because 'there was nothing to do' and 'when people were bored' they were likely to 'get you'. One pupil thought it 'unfair' that some people were stronger than others and did not cry because crying 'always got you bullied'.

On balance pupils didn't feel that bullying was handled well in schools: whilst there were clear guidelines for 'trivial' things like 'uniform' and you knew 'what you'd get' (as punishment), this was often not the case with bullying. Even in schools that had policies pupils were unable to explain the systems or were unaware of them. In some cases this was also true of teachers. One senior manager knew 'we don't approve of it' (bullying) but couldn't 'tell you the policy off the top of my head'. One head of year said, 'We must have a policy because we've just had Ofsted but I'm not sure what it says.'

Children knew it was wrong and you 'got done' if you were caught, but because there was no clear process there was no sense of duty to the system or to each other. Worse still, because the system was unclear, pupils felt none of the safety or support that a clear policy could offer. The outcome they felt was likely to be that bullying would go unreported both by the victims or the bystanders. For pupils to feel safe and by implication less likely to truant respondents felt:

- The most important thing was for schools to have a clear policy on bullying.
- The policy should be made known to pupils, parents and teachers with regular reminders.
- Clear procedures should be made known to all pupils, parents and teachers and a consistent programme of monitoring and reinforcing the system should be in place.
- Imperfections could be worked out in operation and would do less harm than having no policy at all.

As part of the discussion on policy the author spent some time considering the role of the bystander in the process. It was put to the children that they had a duty to tell the teacher if they knew that bullying was taking place. The response of the children to this view was cautious and illuminating. Some were openly hostile to the view, saying it was unfair and those teachers who expressed such views were unfair. On closer examination their reluctance revealed soundly-based and entirely reasonable objections in the light of some schools' policies.

In short, the concept of a neutral bystander who could 'report' incidents of bullying proved unfounded. Bystanders are involved passively in what they observe and are frightened of active involvement (telling) because of the consequences. They simply have more faith in the bully's ability to deal with the 'grass' than they have in the school's ability to deal with the situation. If, say the children, the school can ask, 'Why didn't you tell?', the child has an equal right to ask, 'Why didn't you (the school) have a system that deals with these things and makes me feel safe enough to report incidents?' Schools cannot with any justification expect a pupil to lead this situation. In this sense schools reflect society: e.g. drug-related crimes of violence in inner cities often go unsolved because people will not inform. The drug dealers have a better system for dealing with problems than the police. For the bystander there is no moral dilemma, it is a question of self-preservation. Only when the school or society can offer adequate processes of protection will we be able to expect more intervention from the bystander.

Whilst it is not the remit of this book to offer specific advice on dealing with bullying one thing does seem clear. Any school hoping to reduce the causative factors of truancy must develop a comprehensive policy dealing with pupil safety (including bullying) in order to create a strong sense of identity with the school community and a sense of well-being for its members.

Stating the school's values and ethos

Before an institution as large and as complex as a school can be managed effectively, it must have a clear identity in the eyes all those involved. It is impossible to ask staff pupils, governors or anyone else to commit themselves to a school if they do not understand what that school stands for and to what, in consequence, they are committing themselves.

The establishment of a school identity is a long and often costly process that requires constant review and update. Whilst schools may enjoy a certain reputation in their neighbourhood, in reality such reputations are based on historical evidence and do not necessarily relate to the present. In an organization where up to 20 per cent of the consumers leave on an annual basis and staff changes are unpredictable there can be no real sense of permanence without constant reinforcement. Paradoxically therefore it is often only possible for schools to go forward by revisiting and reviewing the past.

Who do we involve?

The short answer to this question is everybody. If we are to create a real sense of community in a school then we must recognize the rights and opinions of every member of that community. It is only by feeling that they are valued and have the opportunity to contribute that pupils will identify with the school process.

The structures of a school, like those of the society they should reflect, cannot successfully be imposed by edict. Such a course would promote disaffection, not prevent it. Consequently discussions must involve pupils, teachers, classroom assistants, parents, governors, midday assistants, clerical staff, caretaking staff, education welfare workers, Connexions and any other agency that has a regular input into the school. Although schools should value independent thought and the rights of the individual, there is no room for a private agenda. Only by the creation of an ethos to which everyone subscribes can we work towards the consistency that will promote inclusion.

Promoting a sense of safety

Areas of the curriculum where pupils can be most obviously involved in discussion of policy and the preparation of materials for consideration by parents might include PSHE/citizenship, drama and tutor periods. Activities relating to truancy in such lessons might include questionnaires to obtain pupils' views of the school and to identify areas of anxiety. Schools may also choose to consider friendship projects in forms or year groups that deal with responsibilities, talents, loyalty, etc. and can be applied to a code of respect for others or a policy on bullying.

Surveys inviting children to identify areas of 'high risk' of bullying on a school map or times of 'high risk' on a timetable will provide useful planning information.

Areas of concern

Pupils often identify school toilets as a source of anxiety. Not only do they represent a threat to some pupils, because older children and smokers congregate there, they are also seen as unpleasant or degrading. As part of his own research the author identified pupils who were adamant that they would 'never use the toilets in school.' In their view they were 'smelly, dirty and unpleasant.' Some of the pupils interviewed said that they never normally broke school rules but admitted that at times they had left the school site, without permission, so that they could go home or to a local café and use the toilet facilities.

In the view of these pupils, school would be a better place if the toilets were refurbished, regularly decorated and made part of staff duty patrols instead of being seen as no-go areas. In one primary school this task had been entrusted to the pupil council. As part of the process pupils' views had been canvassed, and the council had liased with the LEA, the caretaker and parents. They had interviewed sales representatives, applied for a grant from the PTA and received money from the building budget.

The general consensus was that the toilets were far more pleasant and that they would be kept that way by an inspection rota of children from each class who checked the condition of the toilets and reported back to the council. Such initiatives seem a small price to pay if the outcome is raised self-esteem amongst pupils and a belief that the school values every member of the community.

Systematized approaches

Activities that systematize approaches have been shown to reduce bullying in some schools by up to 50 per cent, and have led to a consequent reduction in truancy. Zoning the playground will stop the disproportionate use of space by some games and reduce the clashes thus generated. Further zoning of the school grounds will provide quiet areas and 'safe' areas for different age groups and personalities and will enhance many pupils' sense of well-being around the school.

Seated areas are seen by children as a privilege and are enjoyed. Care should be taken however to ensure that they remain places to interact socially and not part of a bullying structure where the more dominant lay territorial claims. Adequate and appropriate provision after discussion with pupils and adequate supervision will reduce danger.

N.B.: Outside seating too close to a building can attract vandals and trespassing outside school hours and may also encourage access to the roof, thereby compromising security.

Play leaders

During a pupil's school life, breaks or lunchtimes take up about 20 per cent of their time. Not surprisingly it is this unstructured time that most often causes anxiety or becomes the focus of unruly behaviour. In some schools for example it has been noted that bullying and confrontation have been considerably reduced by the abandonment of an afternoon break.

Whilst this information is in itself interesting it cannot provide the whole solution because children need some free time for both relaxation and refreshment when they are at school. The solution chosen by some primary schools, often as part of their 'changes to the workforce', has been to appoint a part-time play leader. The role of the play leader is to work with the children, often starting with the infants, to develop play activities during break or lunchtime. As part of the programme, often in concert with the pupil council and the parents, the play leader introduces the children to games and play activities. Often as part of the programme the playground is marked out for games like hopscotch or chess in order to facilitate play. Not only does such a programme take away the boredom that some children feel at break times, but it also gives more insular children the chance to join in and teaches all the children better cooperation and social skills.

In secondary schools this scheme has been adapted to allow for the employment of staff to organize clubs and social activities.

Wider staff involvement

Having said that all staff members are important in raising awareness, midday assistants (MDAs) are often overlooked or given inadequate training. Their role at lunchtimes is to supervise a 'danger time' in the school day. The atmosphere of care they engender has been shown to influence bullying behaviour and create a sense of being 'cared for' which influences against truancy.

Many schools give a low priority to training this group of staff, yet for approximately 15 per cent of the school day they represent the first point of contact with children and are expected to emphasize official school policy whilst handling often difficult situations. Schools must be prepared to finance a programme of training for these staff members and to involve them in the policy-making process. When midday assistants begin work at the school they should be made aware of their job description and should embark upon a period of induction. Shadowing a more experienced colleague will enable to them to get to know the children and give them guidance on the best way to handle various situations.

The details of the MDAs' job description should be agreed between them and the senior management of the school. It should reflect the standards of the school and should make clear the role that an MDA is expected to fulfil. MDAs should have a clear route for referring any incidents to their line manager and should always have immediate access to a member of the senior management team should more serious incidents arise. They should be involved in regular training and meetings to support them in their concerns about aggression, behaviour, swearing, etc, and should be shown that there are a variety of ways of managing behaviour and be made aware of the correct school procedures and sanctions.

Raising the awareness of MDAs through meetings with outside speakers and discussions with teachers will make them better able to appreciate children's needs. By valuing the contribution of the MDAs, relationships within the school will be improved. Pupils will feel valued, they should feel more secure and there should be a consequent improvement in behaviour and a reduction in incidents that might prompt truancy.

Passing the message on

Increase pupils' knowledge of MDAs by issuing name badges and/ or by having their photographs and names on display, in alphabetical order, at some prominent point in the school. The ideal place for this would be on a display board bearing pictures of all staff members, clearly demonstrating that MDAs are an integral part of the school. This same principle should be applied to all other support staff within the school and there should be a clear expectation that pupils give the same respect when addressing all members of the school community.

School councils

Changes to the National Curriculum in 2000 made inclusion a central issue and schools in England and Wales could have no doubt about the intentions of the British Government when they read, in the foreword to the revised National Curriculum, statements such as: 'This National Curriculum includes, for the first time, a detailed overarching statement on inclusion ... to ensure that all pupils have the chance to succeed ... '

This emphasis on inclusion was very much epitomized by the inclusion of PSHE citizenship in the curriculum in response to the findings of 'The Advisory Group for Citizenship and Teaching of Democracy in Schools'. The group, set up in 1997 with Professor Bernard Crick in the chair, was firm in its belief that a wider emphasis should be placed upon relationships, diversity, self-esteem, family and a variety of other 'common values that underpin our schools'. The group went on to express the view that the teaching of PSHE citizenship would enhance learning, improve behaviour and help young people to identify with the education process. Professor Crick firmly endorsed one method of achieving this end when he said: 'School Councils and Class Councils are an obvious sign that a school takes Citizenship seriously.' By including class councils in this statement Crick was acknowledging the valuable contribution of classroom-based democracy that can be operated in secondary school or in primary schools, possibly through circle time, as a precursor to the introduction of a full school council. This implicit reference to circle time, in particular, underlines once again the importance that should be attached to early intervention.

It is widely agreed that the operation of school councils brings great benefit to schools, and in the US and Canada (amongst others) they have been an integral part of education for some time. In a letter to Baroness Ashton at the DfES in 2002, Brian Simpson MEP (Member of the European Parliament) pointed out that, amongst the membership of the European Union at that time, 'The UK is the only country within the Union that is not required by law to have a School Council.' Included amongst the many benefits brought by a school council and directly relevant to improving attendance are:

- An aid to inclusion
- Improved attendance
- Improved discipline and behaviour
- Enhanced relationships between *all* members of the school community
- Improved social and learning environment for pupils
- Enhanced primary–secondary transfer
- Improved confidence and self-esteem for pupils
- Improved school self-evaluation

The creative use of the council will allow schools to make a change in the relationship between staff and pupils. The ability to make decisions about the school and their future confers ownership upon the pupils, removes the possibility of confrontation over rules and helps the pupils to gain a working knowledge of how and why some decisions are made.

Similarly, by giving all staff – whether teaching, support, maintenance or clerical – the opportunity to approach the pupils about an issue, through the school council, matters can be dealt with in an atmosphere of understanding before they become an issue.

Research evidence

In a report entitled 'School Councils and Pupil Exclusions' prepared by Professor Lyn Davies for School Councils UK, the relationship between school councils and levels of pupil exclusion was examined.

Ten state schools from across England from both urban and rural locations and from different socio-economic backgrounds were selected for study. All the schools had systems of pupil democracy in operation and all had low or declining levels of exclusion. The main aim of the research was to discover whether, by giving pupils a democratic voice in the management of their school, improved behaviour and a reduction in fixed term and permanent exclusions could be achieved.

In general, headteachers, teachers and support staff were positive about the impact, or the potential impact, of a school council, and felt that it was a central tool in the management of behaviour. This view was voiced particularly strongly in primary schools. The pupil councillors themselves were unanimously enthusiastic about their role and enjoyed the responsibility and sense of being able to contribute. However, the majority of pupils were unsure about the effects of the school council. Some felt the council was important for dealing with issues such as bullying, whilst others felt that the council did not tackle important enough issues or did not have the power to change things. Such ambivalence gives clear messages about the need to support school councils through class councils in order to ensure a feeling of direct involvement for all pupils.

Ofsted, for their part, felt that school councils played a very important role, and the study concluded that school councils could help to reduce exclusions in a number of ways:

Direct impact through:
- Peer control or monitoring of individual children at risk of exclusion.
- Socializing into the norms of behaviour.
- Peer support or advocacy for individual children.
- Enabling bullying or other problems to be shared.

Semi-direct impact through:
- Generating codes of conduct and anti-bullying policies, which are seen as owned by the pupils.
- Pupil-inspired ideas to minimize behaviours associated with exclusion, particularly with regard to
- Creating an adult, dignified and caring environment.

Indirect impact through:
Conveying to pupils and parents the powerful messages that:

- Children are listened to and are treated with respect.
- Children should 'look out' for each other and be able to express grievances.
- Problems can be sorted out.

A number of dilemmas or watch points were also revealed during the research, centred around:

- The 'representativeness' of pupil councillors.
- The ambiguous role of a pupil councillor.
- The need for full support by teachers.
- The need for a supporting structure of class, year or tutor

group councils, or circle time, to involve all pupils in the
school.

- The potentially punitive strategies devised by pupils.
- The frequency and timing of meetings.
- The need for a wide-ranging agenda.
- The need to constantly review and revisit school policies.
- Over-dependence on school councils, and transitions to the
  next level of schooling.

School councils, it should be stressed, cannot be seen in isolation
from a number of other key strategies and structures in a school,
and will interact with these in varied ways to promote inclusion.
These include:

- Achievement and target setting.
- Pastoral and mentoring systems.
- Rewards and sanction systems.
- Active equal opportunities policies.
- Other forms of pupil gathering to foster solidarity.

Overall, the report recommends school councils or circle time as
being a particularly significant part of the raft of measures that a
school takes to promote a sense of ownership, and therefore
inclusion, in a school. It further concluded that a school council
may be one of the most cost-effective ways of developing
inclusion and of recognizing pupil potential.

Behaviour

Directly connected to school councils is the issue of behaviour in
our schools. The notion of codes of conduct and the rejection of
'control' by absentees is often cited as a major factor when dealing
with improved attendance.

The research by Professor Davies found that schools held the
view that they emphasized positive rather than negative discipline.
Pupils, however, even though they had had some involvement in
creating the code of conduct, differed in their views about how
much praise was offered and generally seemed able to identify a
larger number of 'don'ts' than 'dos' when commenting on their
schools' behaviour policies.

Evolving a code of conduct

The starting point for any code of conduct should be the notion that everyone – pupils, teachers, parents and support staff – has an equal role to play in achieving the common goal of creating an effective school community that offers the opportunity for everyone to achieve their potential. There should be no sense of hierarchy in the system where, for example, the 'clever' academic children are seen to be more valued than those pupils who are more 'practically' or 'vocationally' orientated. Within an effective code of conduct the poor attender should receive the same quality of attention as the pupil in regular attendance.

Schools should encourage all concerned to broaden concepts and to be flexible in their views. The aims of the school should be clearly stated, and enshrined in underpinning principles rather than in a long list of specific rules. Three or four such principles should be enough to cover most contingencies. A small number is easy to recall and easy to pass on. They are easy to publicize and can be made prominent throughout the school. Rules for acceptable behaviour follow naturally from principles. Their relationship with the accessible principles helps pupils to see their relevance and enhances the feeling of caring in the school both for the community and for the individuals that make up that community.

By using principles as the baseline it is possible to be consistent with major issues yet reserve the right to be flexible and to consider circumstances with less vital issues. Since all judgements refer back to the principles there is never a problem with consistency.

Rewards and sanctions

Throughout his own research the author regularly spoke with pupils who expressed their sense of individuality and the need to feel personally cared for. This finding supports the view that rule making should involve the pupils. Where pupils felt they had been consulted and had the chance to discuss things they seemed to be more at ease with the system of discipline and more accepting of the rules. Pupils and their teachers who had been involved in rule-making felt that it was important to agree consistent rewards and sanctions that pupils feel are worthwhile and attainable and relevant and appropriate respectively.

On reflection it seems self-evident, but schools should avoid the example of one 11–16 school visited by the author where a list of 28 'don'ts' and three 'rewards' was displayed in each classroom. The situation was further exacerbated by the fact that the three rewards were hierarchical and the third level could only be achieved by passing through a complex system of points and 'graduating' from the other two.

Research by the SCRE for their 2003 report 'Absence from school' revealed quite widespread use of reward systems to encourage attendance. Generally speaking, attendance competitions were more frequent and popular in primary schools, but were in use in some secondary schools. In his own discussions with pupils the author found systems which rewarded children for good attendance to be very popular. Receiving certificates, prizes and the approval of school and teachers was very important to many children. Of paramount importance, however, was the fairness of the system and many views were expressed on this matter. Children felt that teachers were often inconsistent in applying systems and comments such as 'They all say something different' and 'They don't know what they're doing' revealed a lack of faith in the system. Lateness was often cited as an example of inconsistency, in that a blanket rule was applied in many schools regardless of circumstances.

For their part, teachers often seemed undecided about how to apply certain rules and some were unsure whether it was possible to be consistent *and* flexible when dealing with children. Staff in schools that had adopted a model of 'underpinning principles' when making rules seemed least troubled by this issue and the application of those same standards and principles in subject as well as whole school situations gave a greater sense of consistency.

Nevertheless, the SCRE point out that reward systems can have limited effect in 'reaching "hard-line" poor attenders', and that reward systems were not always sustainable. In some schools it seemed as if children were disillusioned with the reward system, especially those where the ultimate 'reward' was some form of gift. Usually this was because great emphasis had been placed on the gift and less on the honour. The end result was that children expected too much and were disappointed. This was not the case where the reward was clearly a symbol and the real achievement was to be seen as worthy of reward.

Pupils were additionally concerned that the nature of some schemes meant that they or their class could never win. One pupil pointed out to the author that the opportunity to succeed lay either with the academically gifted, or with the very poor who had improved. Naturally the end result is that the majority, despite always behaving, attending and working (without necessarily shining) can never expect to be rewarded for what they achieved.

The likelihood is that those who already have a tendency towards truanting behaviour will relish the opportunity given to them by this system, since it reinforces the alienation that they already feel. The solution is to make the system more inclusive by widening the range of approved behaviour and rewarding pupils according to their potential and according to service in extra-curriculum activities. The obstacle to such a strategy, noted by the SCRE, is the amount of time it requires for its introduction and administration, so school managers will have to make clear decisions about where their priorities lie and about the investment of resources.

Traveller children, EAL children and asylum seeker children

In its most recent guidance on inspections Ofsted has recognized and inspectors are now required to evaluate

'how effectively the school inducts new pupils and ensures the needs of particular pupils are being met, for example, by supporting refugee children and recognizing the effect of their education being interrupted.'

They further state, and here they refer to all parents, that the school should: '... draw in parents who find it difficult to approach school.'

For many years schools in some areas of England and Wales have been accustomed to accommodating the children of traveller families as they pass through the area on their traditional route. Similarly schools, most frequently though not exclusively, in urban areas have received and educated children from indigenous families where English is not the first language. Understandably the ability of an individual school to deal with such contingencies has affected the quality of education received and the willingness of the children to identify with or attend the school.

The advice of Ofsted and British Government policies relating to refugee status families and their dispersal throughout England and Wales, means that many more schools are now required to offer education to asylum seekers and the quality of that provision has been brought sharply into focus.

Traveller children

Traveller children are, by virtue of their culture, nomadic. They have ethnic and cultural rights and these are reflected in the regulations relating to their attendance at school. Travellers must attend 200 school sessions in an academic year, though in truth these are not usually made. Their absence, provided they are expected to return to the school, should be recorded as authorized and marked with the appropriate code (see Chapter 2).

In the majority of cases matters relating to the education of traveller children concern primary schools, since travellers do not readily achieve transfer. They are wary of the 'big school' and its influences. There is an element of fear that the school will educate children out of their culture. Once a traveller child has received basic education up to the age of eleven their parents normally prefer to organize education at home. In truth, after the age of eleven, traveller children become part of the economic unit of the family. Boys are expected to learn the family trade and girls become carers and homemakers.

Recording attendance and progress

Changes to the criminal justice act have made it easier to block access to or move travellers on from their traditional sites. There are now fewer local authority transit sites and travellers are reduced to using wasteland or car parks when they stay in a particular area. Not only does this reinforce the mistaken stereotype of the 'dirty gypsy', but it means that their stay in an area might be cut short and school attendance will consequently be affected.

Green cards and red books

One problem that traveller children and schools face is the monitoring of progress. In an attempt to create a coherent record a system of green cards was created. The idea was that each traveller child would be issued with a card, which would be their 'passport' to school and would carry an up-to-date record of their progress. Some families were very keen on the idea but others thought it was 'spying'. In practice, because of their erratic lifestyle some families had more than one green card and none contained a full record of the child's progress. An attempt to make the system more effective through the introduction of a 'Client Held Record' or Red Book, as it is popularly known, has encountered similar problems. This system, based on a record book containing the pupil's Unique Pupil's Identity Number, has still resulted in traveller pupils holding more than one record and has not prevented the need for constant re-assessment.

Neither EAL nor asylum seeker children are included in this system. EAL pupils are usually resident in one place and asylum seeker children, though mobile, do not move as frequently and the legal position of their families means that their whereabouts are more easily ascertained.

Finance

Should it be necessary for the Education Support Services to find a school place for a traveller or an asylum seeker child, the time of year can be crucial. The tightness of most school budgets and the way in which finance is allocated means that many schools have to be ever watchful of the time and resources they have to commit to the children in their care. The simple fact is that placing a child in a school the week before PLASC (Pupil Level Annual School Census, still referred to as Form 7 in some areas) is submitted will often be easier than placing a child the week after. By the same token schools in receipt of extra grants to protect their small school status are wary of the impact that additional numbers will have on their budget.

What support is available?

The way in which schools receive finance to support traveller, EAL and asylum seeker children varies according to the numbers involved and the policy of the LEA. On a statutory basis asylum seeker children are entitled to free school meals, a grant of £25 towards school uniform and a further grant of £500 to assist with specialist support. The latter funding is either devolved directly to schools or, in some authorities, finances the specialist input of an ESS (Education Support Service). Even where specialist support is available authorities can usually only offer sufficient teaching support to develop basic social language for non-English speaking pupils. The development of academic language has to be left to the school and funding changes planned for 2006 mean that even more responsibility will rest with them as funding is devolved from the LEAs. Schools will have no alternative other than to offer this support and their exact role will be defined by the British Government initiative (currently being piloted in some areas), 'Aiming High – Raising the Achievement of Ethnic Minority Pupils.'

Other support that an ESS team can offer will depend on local circumstances at the time. Any budget is finite and since support for a changing school population is reactive rather than proactive funding has to be managed to allow for the various contingencies which might arise during the academic year.

School performance

Irrespective of finance there are other issues surrounding the inclusion of traveller, EAL and asylum seeker children that schools have to address. If, and this cannot be known in advance, a pupil records 50 per cent attendance then they are a detriment to the school's performance figures. If, on the other hand, they have a 98 per cent attendance record then they are an asset. One pupil in a class of thirty represents 3.3 per cent of the cohort. In the case of both attendance and academic performance a child who does not attend a school but appears on the roll can radically affect performance figures. There is no doubt that some schools would see this as a problem. Despite the fact that figures for the performance of asylum seeker children need not be reported officially for two years, they are still reported to the LEA. Some schools remain fearful that they will be judged, at least on a local level, and management teams must seek reassurance on that matter from the authority.

In the final analysis however there can only be one answer and that is that the rights of the child, regardless of background, must be paramount. Schools that embrace this view will have the best opportunity to promote good attendance and thereby improve the achievement of all the children on their roll.

Cultural issues

Apart from lifestyle choices already referred to there are other cultural issues associated with traveller, EAL and asylum seeker children. A lack of uniform, 'acceptable' hairstyles, earrings and other piercings are just a few of the issues that some schools find difficult to accommodate. Whilst most schools see the enriching value of children from other cultures, some can be inflexible, insisting that the LEA supplies a uniform or that potential pupils should change their appearance before they are admitted. Such schools inevitably have to review their equal opportunities policies and it is almost invariably those schools with the most flexible codes of conduct (see Chapter 7) that most readily assimilate pupils from other cultures.

Multi-cultural education

Schools, irrespective of the area in which they are situated or the ethnic composition of their intake, must have a multicultural policy in existence and this should be reflected in the life and the curriculum of the school. The key question is: will children and their parents, regardless of background, feel welcomed and valued by the school? It is not sufficient for schools to claim to be multicultural because they serve the occasional Indian meal at lunchtime or because they cover slavery in history. True multicultural education goes beyond tokenism. It should be ingrained in the life of the school and should reflect the history and culture of all the ethnic groups that make up our society, taking a positive view of their lifestyles and celebrating the diversity, enrichment and understanding that they can bring to our lives.

Furthermore, schools must acknowledge and address the nature of discriminatory behaviour that exists in our schools. In the case of asylum seeker children, indigenous EAL children and other minority groups, those from Africa and Asia often face more barriers because they are more easily identifiable. Even amongst teachers dealing with non-English speaking pupils, research has revealed that there exists a hierarchy of languages. In the first instance non-English speaking pupils are often assumed to have special needs and, even after assessment, those whose first language is European are thought to be more 'intelligent' than those from areas such as Asia or the Middle East.

Barriers to education and inclusion for ethnic minority children
There is no doubt that some areas of the curriculum and some aspects of school life are barriers to inclusion and may even encourage non-attendance. Religious education, sex education, health education and physical education present the most obvious barriers, but even the school canteen can present problems. Providing free school meals for children from ethnic minorities (asylum seeker children automatically have that entitlement) is only an effective aid to inclusion if the meals provided respect dietary practices specified by religion and culture.

In certain societies where the male is central to the family and other social structures it may be hard for parents to understand and acknowledge the authority of a female teacher. The solutions to these and other problems will only come through the development of effect multicultural and equal opportunities policies, and schools have the right to expect that the development of such policies will be strongly supported by the LEA. Many LEAs through their EAL service offer a range of translated letters in various languages to aid communication with parents and pupils. Those who do not use national agencies, and some of these are listed in Appendix C.

Learning the language, translators and interpreters
It is generally accepted that it takes between two and seven years for a child to achieve competence in a language, yet the National Curriculum in England and Wales continues to set targets for children with little or no allowance for language ability. One way of improving communication is through the use of interpreters, but this is expensive and problematical given the range of languages a school might need to access. Telephone translation

services can prove to be impersonal and, given that some are based abroad, may prove costly.

Practical steps for communication

Where possible, schools are advised to use their local EAL services or to contact the organizations listed in Appendix C. Through these agencies contact can often be made with bilingual members of minority communities prepared to offer help. Other willing helpers can often be found at the mosque, the temple, the local community centre, etc. As part of their community role Connexions offers support to asylum seekers through their 'Positive Futures' programme, and in many areas the police and EWS employ specialist community liaison workers.

Without this ethnic community support, schools who have successfully integrated additional language children and supported their language development sometimes find that they have a consequent attendance problem. The legal status of asylum seeking families often requires them to attend Home Office interviews and other meetings related to their presence in the country. In the absence of any other language support the families turn to their children to act as interpreters and once again the importance of supporting pupil *and* parent when developing good attendance is illustrated.

Conclusion

By investing the time to involve all the interested parties in the policy-making process they will, in time, become embedded in the ethos of the school. If the starting point is that the 'critical mass' is balanced in favour of truancy and disaffection then that mass will have to be eroded before progress is made. Like water dripping on a stone, constant reinforcement of a policy wears away resistance. Ultimately, standards related to attendance, safety, respect, etc. become part of the general ethos of the school and all children and parents become aware of it.

Relatively small and straightforward changes, like the introduction of an electronic registration system, can be used to achieve this change of ethos. Take the register in individual lessons as well as in form time and pass comments to the children. Ask them about school clubs, remark on their recovery if they have been absent, etc. Children respond well to the idea that they are personally noticed and are less likely to become resentful. They are also aware of who takes regular registers and where the scope for truancy is greatest.

Our role as teachers is to open the doorway of understanding to all members of the school community. Like all doorways there will be times when we must go first and times when we step back and let our companions go first. There may even be times when both will turn sideways and pass through together. Our professionalism will help us to judge what is appropriate and will enable us to encourage good attendance by creating the safe, inclusive and caring environment that all members of the school community have the right to enjoy.

8 Alternative Approaches and Support Systems

'If there is anything that we wish to change in the child, we should first examine and see whether it is not something that could be better changed in ourselves.' (*Carl Gustav Jung*)

Motivating pupils to achieve the best that they are capable of achieving is a central concern for every school. As teachers we want our pupils to succeed both out of a sense of professional pride as well as in the hope that this success will afford the young people choices and opportunities that they otherwise might not have had. To this end it is not uncommon for school corridors and classrooms to be adorned with quotes and mottoes which will provide food for thought and, hopefully, shape good learning attitudes. Popular amongst these ubiquitous mottoes is:

'If you only do what you do, you'll only get what you've got.'

Simplistic as it may be it is, nevertheless, difficult to argue against the basic sentiment. However, at the risk of going a motto too far:

'What's sauce for the goose is sauce for the gander.'

If we really are sincere in our desire to help every child succeed then we too must acknowledge the need to change our approach and to innovate. All too often schools offer a standard package to a very non-standard clientele, and those who fail to identify with what is on offer are judged, blamed and rejected.

There are, without doubt, pupils with poor attendance records who are difficult to reach. In their case recourse to legislation and strategies contained elsewhere in this book may be the only option: but what of that much larger group of pupils who want to succeed but also want the right to question and to establish their own individuality? A standard response to these pupils may well push them further away from school and exacerbate rather than solve the problem. Perhaps in these cases we should acknowledge that some disaffection is in fact healthy and attempt to accommodate rather than stifle it.

Disaffection, a common and positive trait

If schools are to prepare young people for the real world then they must reflect the real world, and equip pupils with the appropriate skills to live full lives and to make worthwhile contributions. Inescapably, within that real world, disaffection exists and provided its expression remains appropriate, it is seen as healthy and acceptable. Not too many years ago, the mere thought that we should question the role of the royal family would have caused outrage. More recently, however, that outrage has assumed a different focus and items published in all branches of the media questioning the status quo have revealed the increasing role that public opinion has to play in our lives.

The disaffection of the masses in reshaping opinion, controlling fuel prices, opposing a war, fighting for the environment, etc. has become a part of our everyday life. Indeed, by giving it the less emotive name 'public opinion', it has become an acceptable social mechanism. Throughout the world we can find examples of the disaffected being 'rehabilitated' and graduating to government. One man's 'terrorist' is another man's 'freedom fighter', and nowhere has this truth been more evident than in the Republic of South Africa. These facts notwithstanding it is, nevertheless, difficult for teachers to associate the courage and vision of Nelson Mandela with the aberrant behaviour of a disruptive pupil and, apart from pondering its humorous possibilities, the proposition is unlikely to attract further attention.

The fact remains, however, that the problem of disruptive and disaffected pupils exists in our schools and perhaps the only way of addressing the problem is to review our perceptions of what disaffection is and who the disaffected are. Given that disaffection is, in some senses, a social mechanism the view that such pupils can be dismissed as 'unworthy' would seem inappropriate. Additionally, since schools have a duty (both legal and moral) to all children, the 'disaffected' have as much right to our positive attention as the 'well-behaved' pupils.

In addressing disaffection the first part of the process must be to objectively review the institutions that are being questioned, whilst at the same time actively identifying positive traits in the pupils who are posing those questions.

For many pupils school is a place where all sense of choice has been removed. In most cases the school has been selected on the basis of where parents live and what they think will be 'good' for their children. On arrival in the school children are presented with a set of rules designed, not for them as individuals, but for past pupils and by teachers whose main priority was to ensure control in school and to conduct lessons without a fuss. If, under these circumstances, pupils don't feel personally involved with the rules we can hardly be surprised. If we add to this the fact that the values enshrined in school rules represent an alien land to some children then questioning on their part would seem inevitable.

As teachers we must constantly ask ourselves what the rules are for. Are they for the children or do they simply represent points of reference for the teachers? Do we always keep certain rules because they are relevant or are we simply maintaining tradition? Do we ensure that pupils understand rules and that their relevance is made clear? Children who question our standards in school by showing disaffection are often dismissed as worthless, beyond redemption, etc. They build up a reputation and, by self-fulfilling prophecy, often continue to be disaffected throughout their school lives. In some cases, it may be true that a child's behaviour is outrageous. In other cases, however, it may be just as true that our outrage is not at the behaviour but at the fact that the behaviour attacks the 'sacred cow' that represents our identity and our raison d'être. We must ask ourselves why it is that children have to accept our values, wholeheartedly, all of the time. Why is it that our systems will not stand examination and are not open to change or flexibility?

Many of the children we see as failures or disaffected in school enjoy success in their own terms when they leave. They have jobs, they have friends, they are loved and trusted, exchange opinions, tell jokes, take holidays and do the myriad other things that make up a normal everyday life. True they may have 'changed' since they left school, they may have 'grown up' (and some will admit that themselves), but the potential was there previously. What was it in school that stopped us from seeing the virtues their friends discovered? What was it about school that stopped them from growing up and prevented them from celebrating their right to be different?

Having accepted that 'lost sheep' can achieve success, it is appropriate for teachers now to look to themselves. Even amongst teachers there are those who did not like school. The jaundiced few may say: why should they? School, after all, is a place with too few toilets and too many rules, that is usually too hot in summer and too cold in winter. How many people, given a free choice, would be motivated to work (without pay) in such a factory? Add to this the poor meals and the requirement to stand outside in the cold for up to an hour a day and there is little to recommend it. The difference, for most teachers, is that they found a way through the disadvantages. They had the ability to succeed and to select those areas that gave them the most satisfaction. Their success became their passport, and often misdemeanours were overlooked in deference to their success.

Looking back over our lives as pupils, students and teachers we have to ask: how many of us were truants? How many missed homework or assignment deadlines? How many did not listen in particular lessons or did not even bother attending certain lectures? Many teachers will see examples of their own behaviour in these questions and even today we continue to practise avoidance tactics in our employment. Many of us, prior to the staff meeting that we do not relish, will finish our coffee or take that 'important' phone call. We finish conversations (not always important ones) and arrive late for lessons. We attend inset days and 'switch off' halfway through when we decide the speaker has nothing to offer. The justification is simple: we are professionals and we can make judgements where the children cannot.

In our private lives we continue our disaffection by objecting to processes around us. It may be by paying our direct debit to 'Greenpeace', knowing that they will disrupt nuclear testing, etc. It may be a donation to 'Compassion in World Farming' knowing that they will blockade the ports to stop the export of veal calves; or it may simply be that we only pay our bills on final demand to protest at the payrise of the company chairman. Disaffection is normal. It is part and parcel of our everyday lives. We commit acts of disaffection or we 'elect' organizations to speak for us just as some children defer to more eloquent or more confident classmates. The difference is simply that we protest from a point of power and through channels that we recognize as socially acceptable.

There is, in the final analysis, no reason why we should not accord pupils the same privileges. No one is suggesting that we should offer pupils the right to reject. Indeed if we leave them until they reject it is too late. Surely it is preferable to allow children to question and recognize it for what it is, a normal and healthy process? By giving children channels by which they can question in school we will reduce disaffection. Children will feel ownership of the system, proud of their rights as individuals and able to take decisions and make compromises that will shape their future.

Children who are not heeded will inevitably become like the baby who needs changing. By responding to the whimper and fulfilling the child's needs we control the behaviour. If we ignore the plea, the whimper very soon becomes a scream and placating the child becomes a far more considerable problem.

Other methods of supporting pupils

As well as creating democracy and increasing communication in schools, there are a number of other methods that can be used to support pupils in addition to those already mentioned. Included amongst them might be the school's existing pastoral system. However, to many of those pupils who already feel alienated by school, this system may be too closely associated with the 'establishment' and it may well be necessary to turn to other agencies.

The existence of Connexions offers secondary schools a readily available system of counselling, and specific examples of their work are outlined in the case study of South Bromsgrove High School (See Chapter 9). More general guidelines for their role were drawn up in the summer of 2002 as part of a joint initiative with the DfES and Local Authority Education Welfare Services.

Details of these guidelines, which relate directly to truancy, can be found in Appendix D. Additionally some or all of the following services, (in no particular order) may prove useful to schools:

- *The Education Welfare Service.* Mentioned elsewhere, this service not only pursues cases of absence but often provides or facilitates access to other services, some of which are mentioned below.
- *Community Safety Partnerships.* Usually multi-agency groups which offer access to probation services, social workers, community police services, victim support, parenting initiatives, etc. These local authority based groups usually have the infrastructure, and sometimes the funding, to provide support for schools, pupils and parents through visits to schools, mentoring and various other schemes that raise awareness, promote community confidence and discourage non-attendance.
- *Youth Offending Service.* Although an autonomous service, this agency tends to work closely with others to discourage offending behaviour, bring about prosecutions where necessary and to seek orders that will rehabilitate young people and maintain their link with education. An example of a specific project is given in Chapter 6 and an outline of their work is included in Chapter 9.
- *Education Psychologists.* Schools have had a longstanding relationship with this service. Often their resources are heavily in demand, but the use of these professionals can prove invaluable in identifying and addressing issues that contribute to non-attendance.
- *Child and Adolescent Mental Health Service (CAMHS).* This service is usually based in a department of the local hospital. Although there is often a waiting list, the service offers valuable support to non-attenders whose behaviour might be emotionally and/or psychologically rooted. Access to this service is usually achieved through the Education Welfare Department. Referral can also be made through a child's GP. In either case it will be important to create a relationship with the parent or the carer if any referral is to succeed.
- *Pupil Counsellors.* Some schools employ counsellors on a

permanent basis to assist with advice and support for pupils. These counsellors are often youth workers and have an opportunity to meet with the pupils in circumstances other than school. Their role is confidential (as far as the law will allow) and though they might well communicate a pupil's concerns to the school it is important that the pupils see them as separate to the general structure and management systems.

- *Peer Counsellors.* Many schools have successfully introduced the idea of peer mentors at primary and secondary level. The work of these pupils varies enormously and they can be responsible for a range of initiatives designed to make school a more enjoyable and less threatening experience. Some of theses roles include being 'buddies' to younger children, bullying mediators, administrators of restorative justice, volunteers on the 'friendship bench' and learning partners for EAL or other special needs children. There is a range of information available through, amongst others, the EWS, School Councils UK and in books on circle time by writers such as Jenny Moseley.

- *Learning Mentors.* This initiative, financed originally in some areas by Excellence in Cities grants, has offered effective support to pupils facing problems. Although specific grants are not available to every school, many are taking advantage of the 'restructuring of the workforce' to introduce support staff in this capacity.

Classroom management, missed opportunities

Although the actual names have been changed the following is an accurate reproduction of a report, prepared by a special needs teacher, recording the behaviour of a pupil in an English lesson. The report was passed to the head of year with the expectation that Daniel, the pupil who is the subject of the report, would be disciplined in some way. Daniel, a Year 9 pupil, had moderate learning difficulties that could, if support was unavailable, translate themselves into poor behaviour. The report of the incident is reproduced in exactly the form it was presented to the head of year.

The incident took place after morning break, between 10.15 am and 11.00 am. Daniel was one of eight pupils. A classroom assistant would normally have supported the teacher, but that help was not available on this occasion. The teacher decided that ignoring Daniel's behaviour was the best way forward and 'recorded every outburst, as it happened, with the minimum of comment.'

There is no intention, on the part of the author, to question the ability or professionalism of the teacher. It is obviously impossible to make a balanced judgement of the incident in isolation. However, the account does prompt certain questions and as well as posing their own questions, readers may wish to consider.

- Did Daniel know what to expect or could he have been prepared more thoroughly for the lesson?
- Did Daniel receive adequate support? Did he have reason to believe that he would be able to succeed/cope with the task?
- Were Daniel's 'avoidance tactics' recognized as such or were they viewed as a more direct challenge to the teacher's authority?
- How early in the process could the teacher have negotiated a way forward?
- Could an attempt at a solution have been made before Daniel used bad language and insulted other pupils?
- Was ignoring Daniel a successful tactic?
- Did keeping a written record of events, without comment, in front of Daniel calm or exacerbate the situation?
- Given the difficulties that Daniel already faces in school, if this situation was to be repeated, how might it affect Daniel's attitude to learning and attendance?
- How might a repetition of this situation affect the teacher's view of Daniel?

It is entirely possible that the situation in this lesson could have been managed differently and that a different approach or different circumstances might have achieved a different outcome. The teacher, without classroom support, was already under pressure. By the time Daniel concedes and makes what is a desperate call for help the teacher has lost patience. Daniel's requests are ignored. His attempt to rescue the situation falls on deaf ears and, rather than taking the opportunity to build a relationship, the teacher decides it is too late and initiates disciplinary proceedings by referring the matter to the head of year.

Daniel's English lesson
'Not English. I thought it was art. I won't work.'
'I haven't got my tray.'
'I won't get my work out. I'm not doing it.'
'I want to go to the toilet.'
'I can't work until I've been to the toilet.'
'I won't work until I've been to the frigging toilet.'
'I won't work until I've been to the frigging bog.'
'This work is s★★t!'

(Told not to use bad language)

'S★★t, f★★k, dildo.'

(Told he would be reported to Mr Houghton)

'Mr Houghton is a dildo.'
'Pamela is a dirty slag!'
'Kelly called me a d★★khead.'

(Matthew went to the toilet. He had asked quietly twice)

'You let Matthew go just to get on my bloody nerves.'
'This school stinks. I don't want to be here.'

(Daniel finally got his books out at 11 a.m., ten minutes before the end of the lesson)

'I need help. I don't understand it.'
'All right I don't want to go the toilet. I just need help.'

(Told teacher busy helping someone else)

I've been much worse with Mrs Lessing than I have been to you.'
'Help me with my work.'
'I can't work because you won't help me.'

9 Supporting Good Attendance through Alternative Approaches

Support mechanisms to encourage good attendance are becoming increasingly common and, as expertise grows, are becoming more specifically tailored to the needs of each school and its individual members.

In 2001 the British Government published, as part of its ongoing commitment to improving attendance, a booklet entitled 'Tackling Truancy Together: Truancy Buster Awards 2001. Case Studies'. The booklet, reference DfES/0084/2001, is available through DfES publications in Nottingham and contains details of 50 successful projects in a range of schools across England. Nineteen of the examples are outlined in some detail, and all have a contact number. Many, though not all, of the strategies are already referred to in this book and include initiatives such as breakfast clubs, improved parental contact, increased safety, etc. The 50 examples span the age ranges and also include work done in special schools.

There is no doubt that all of these projects have achieved considerable success but, and perhaps more importantly, the impetus provided by the Truancy Buster Awards has drawn attention to a host of other successful initiatives in schools across England and Wales.

Case study: South Bromsgrove Community High School

At South Bromsgrove Community High School in Worcestershire the headteacher Phil McTague enthusiastically quotes the words of Nicholas Negroponti from the Massachusetts Institute of Technology, that 'Incrementalism is the death of creativity' and in the same breath just as vehemently rejects the maxim, 'If it isn't broken don't fix it.' Phil claims:

> 'There is always something to change. It is the role of educators to make a difference and schools should not simply tinker at the edges: they should find the courage to do something different and better for young people, irrespective of age, ability or attitude.'

South Bromsgrove Community High School is a large middle school of some 1270 pupils. It has a mixed intake, though part of its catchment area, a council estate of 6000 homes, is the biggest in Worcestershire. Attendance and achievement are above average, with the former currently standing at an average of 92 per cent. Unauthorized absence is recorded at 0.5 per cent.

As a middle school without 'compliant' Year 7 and 8 pupils, South Bromsgrove has to work hard to maintain those figures. The introduction and use of an 'honest' electronic registration system has, according to Phil McTague, 'Reduced the volatility of internal truancy and focused attention on a hard core of regular truants and those parents who take their children on holiday in term time.'

In order to achieve improvements in the school environment, and consequent improvements in attendance, Phil believes that spiritual and moral issues are of central importance: 'Schools', he says, 'should not shy away from dealing with abstract, philosophical issues' if they are to improve. There should be no tension between attitudes towards high achievement and special programmes. Additionally, as well as dealing with the extremes of the continuum, schools must ensure that they cater equally for 'the band in the middle'.

On entering the school pupils are given a 'target grade challenge' based on their KS3 scores. The grades and the pupils' progress are monitored by normal assessment reporting and recording processes. Ann Rickard, the school's SENCO and assistant head, administers the process, which includes a range of rewards for a variety of behaviours – not just academic achievement – including awarding points, certificates and comments in planners. For ease of administration all the staff have laptops which are used to record all positive/negative comments, information for regular parents' meetings and, where relevant, to e-mail parents. One recent innovation, introduced at the request of pupils in modern languages, is a different approach to telephone contact with parents. Pupils were aware that teachers often phone parents to report matters of concern. Whilst accepting that system, pupils asked for the added condition that for each teaching group at least one phone call per week should be positive. The teachers agreed and have noted an extremely positive reaction to the system from pupils of all abilities and their parents.

Interesting as some of these systems are, many will be familiar to teachers of all age groups across England and Wales and, although it is encouraging to have good practice confirmed, of particular interest at South Bromsgrove are the additional support mechanisms that Phil McTague and his staff operate.

Underlying philosophy

It is the firm belief of Phil that if a school focuses on the negative behaviour of its pupils then, ultimately, that is the behaviour that will be reinforced. The view at South Bromsgrove is that the emotional quotient is as important as the intelligence quotient, and on that basis great care is taken to ensure that the emotional well-being of pupils is respected. Children mirror behaviour: 'If you bawl and shout at them that's what you get back.' Instead, children at South Bromsgrove are encouraged to be part of the school community and on that basis feel a sense of belonging to the structures rather than experiencing alienation.

Phil McTague stresses that in achieving this end staff must act corporately. He believes that a united approach on simple things sets the tone. Teachers at the school start from a point of praise. Thus, at the start of a lesson those pupils whose uniform is tidy are congratulated upon their effort and appearance. Any other pupils are invited to comply and they too are praised when that is achieved. Similarly the confrontation over equipment with some pupils is avoided by ensuring that staff always have a drawer full of pens, etc. In this way the opportunity for avoidance or confrontation is removed. If the pupil has a pen, there is no issue. In Phil's view children are disorganized because they have no engagement. Their prime concern with school is to know what is in it for them. Making school a pleasant and safe environment is the first step in breaking the cycle. It gives pupils the opportunity to see the reward and encourages them to attend and take up the wider opportunities that school has to offer.

Additional support structures

Once the academic provision of the school has been put into place it is essential to ensure that every child has the opportunity to access that provision. In keeping with the practice of many schools South Bromsgrove has a wide range of extra curricular activities available for its pupils. These include sports, music, drama, community service and a host of other clubs and societies commonly found in schools throughout England and Wales. Whilst a strong general ethos supported by such activities goes a long way towards achieving inclusion, there are always those pupils who have specific needs and whose individualism must be catered for through a diverse range of additional courses and activities. To this end the school has set up a number of activities to support small but significant numbers of pupils who might otherwise find the challenges of school too daunting.

The Neuro Development Movement programme

For a small group of pupils, each day starts in the school's dance studio with about fifteen minutes of movement. The programme, based upon the work of Sally Goddard-Smythe, was introduced and is supervised by Irene Cunliffe. Irene, a teacher with extensive experience of working with special needs pupils, was brought into the school some time ago, with the specific remit of supporting children who have difficulty in accessing the curriculum. Under the scheme, each pupil, supported by volunteer parents and classroom assistants, takes part in a personal programme of movement designed to improve concentration, flexibility and coordination. The direct benefits of this work are improvements in head and eye movement, and ocular control leading to consequent improvements in reading and writing. At the start of each programme pupils' skills in these areas are assessed and Irene is able to produce impressive evidence of the progress made.

Those taking part in the scheme are from across the age ranges and face a variety of challenges including poor posture, lack of confidence, poor handwriting, problems with memory and poor organizational skills. Each pupil works independently, following their own programme and showing an impressive level of organization in preparing and carrying out their personal movement sequences. All speak enthusiastically about the programme and the benefits it has brought to them. Glen and Adrian from Year 10 would 'recommend it to anyone', whilst Matthew from Year 9 reports that 'it has made him feel more confident.' Zak says the programme has, 'helped him look at himself' and that he feels 'fitter, more confident and calmer in the classroom'. He has no doubt that he will keep it up. Mike and Marcus, again from Year 9, both feel more confident. The former says that he takes on the day 'refreshed', has less fear of new people and new teachers and is more organized, whilst the latter says he has better handwriting and can 'dismiss mickey-taking easier'.

The endorsements of the pupils are borne out by the teachers, who have noticed not only an improvement in presentation skills but an increased preparedness to participate and present work as a result of the enhanced self-esteem brought about by the course.

The listening programme

This programme is based upon the knowledge that the left hemisphere of the brain is responsible for motor skills and information processing. The input mechanism for the left hemisphere is the right ear, and this programme sets out to develop that dominance. The programme consists of eight CDs with tracks of birdsong, water and similar sounds. For fifteen minutes a day the participants listen to the tracks and the repetition improves listening, reduces stress and aids information processing. In tandem with the course, teachers have become more aware that it can be of assistance in getting messages through to children. Boys in particular are visual learners. Most teachers are not, and normally do not consider the point. The use of this course has encouraged teachers to stand on the right of pupils when ideas have to be explained, thereby increasing the possibility that the information will be assimilated.

The handwriting programme

Available to pupils of all abilities, either by teacher referral or on a voluntary basis, this programme supports pupils who feel they have a problem in presenting work. The general view of the teachers is that the results have been 'astonishing', with pupils showing a greater desire to record and present work and an increased willingness to show the method when completing written tasks.

Alternative courses and additional activities

For some pupils accessing the mainstream curriculum, irrespective of the support that they receive, can still present problems. The British Government's provision of vocational qualifications has gone some way to addressing the situation for certain pupils in that it is a genuine attempt to provide more practical courses with clear and direct relevance to the world of work. However, many of these courses are still based upon the GCSE format, and as such continue to present difficulties for some pupils. Amongst those facing difficulties might be pupils whose level of ability makes the format challenging, those who have already been alienated by school structures or those whose erratic attendance makes it difficult for them to access courses predominantly based on classroom learning. To this end, and in keeping with many schools in England and Wales, South Bromsgrove have developed 'link courses' in association with the local technical college. Such courses provide different opportunities for those who have, or potentially have, problems with attendance and broad details of the type of provision are given below.

In addition to the alternative courses South Bromsgrove are also keen to layer a variety of other activities into school life which provide both physical and emotional outlets for the pupils.

Sailing has proved to be very popular with the students at the school, and is available both as part of and in addition to the school timetable. 'Sailing', says Phil McTague, 'uses energy, it builds teamwork and relationships in the students and forges the same bonds with the staff.' Above all it challenges pupils personally. It tests their commitment and, through shared experience, teaches them that it is all right to be afraid and to turn to others for support and assistance.

In similar vein the school has made a huge commitment to the Duke of Edinburgh Award Scheme. The number of students involved is certainly the biggest of any school in England and Wales, and believed to be the biggest of any school in Europe. The teachers are convinced of the importance of such activities and their view is supported by the DfES who agree that such activities can be important aids to building relationships and improving attendance.

Student counselling

As well as contributing to the school's PSHE/citizenship programme Patrick Barker, the school's full-time pastoral care worker, counsels and supports pupils in their learning by helping them to deal with issues of self-esteem, problem-solving and relationships with their parents and their peers. To achieve this worthwhile but complex goal Patrick uses a circular model for his counselling which starts with:

Acceptance, through which pupils learn to appreciate the idea of being accepted for what they *are* rather than what they *do*. From this the pupils move on to the idea of

Sustenance, and learn that people value them for themselves not for the results that they can bring the school or the kudos they can bring to their parents through their achievements. At the next stage pupils learn

Significance, which leads them to say, with pride, 'I am ME.' Having passed through these stages pupils can then turn their attention to

Achievement, and are encouraged to maximize their potential. With each achievement pupils are able to 'travel the circle', again reinforcing their self-esteem and strengthening them-selves, emotionally, for the next challenge.

Despite working closely with the school and its pastoral structures Patrick is keen to ensure that pupils know he is independent. Whilst he may talk about achievement with the pupils, he is concerned primarily with the development of the individual and whilst this will certainly impact upon their welfare in the school, the task of 'progress' chasing falls to the year heads and the form tutors and not to him.

The family unit

Patrick is convinced that the role of the family is central to the work that he does. Indeed he is unequivocal when he says:

> 'More than is generally realized, the role of developing relationships with parents is at least as important, and often makes possible, the counselling and support work with the pupils.'

Early intervention

As with most initiatives associated with improving attendance, early intervention improves the likelihood of success. Patrick starts that process at South Bromsgrove by building relationships with the feeder schools, by working in the local community centre and by involving himself as fully as possible in the process of pupil transfer.

Integrated systems

'Pupils, their achievements, their behaviour and their home lives can never', says Patrick, 'be dealt with in isolation from each other.' On this basis Patrick spends a lot of time offering parenting courses in the school and at the local community centre. The parents of those pupils who have, or potentially have, problems in school are met and offered personal invitations to attend.

The courses, which rely heavily on the work of organizations such as 'Positive Parenting', and the YMCA 'Dads and Lads' project (see below), seek to take a wider view of pupil welfare than simply their behaviour and attendance at school. Courses deal with anger management, developing understanding and emotional security. They examine how parents and children communicate, how appropriate boundaries can be agreed and problems solved.

Of paramount importance is the spirit in which the courses are offered. In Patrick's experience, the imposition of parenting orders by the courts, when children already have acute attendance problems, is 'too little too late' and is often seen by parents and pupils alike as a punishment and, consequently, resented.

'It is counterproductive', says Patrick, 'to suggest to parents that they have failed and need remedial assistance.' What Patrick seeks to achieve is a partnership that celebrates the positive. Patrick enlists the support of parents by inviting them to take part in programmes that will make their children happier, safer, less likely to become involved in offending behaviour and more likely to have the opportunity to enjoy a full and productive life. As a result of his success Patrick is now, in conjunction with the YHA and other locally-based agencies, piloting the idea of residential 'time out' programmes for parents and their children.

Code of conduct and discipline

Over a number of years Mike Ford, the deputy head principally responsible for behaviour management, has developed and refined systems that are viewed as workable and equitable by staff, pupils and parents alike.

As a starting point the school used a Yellis questionnaire to establish pupils' perceptions of the school. Mike feels that this sort of school self-evaluation, as opposed to relying on staff impressions and assumptions, is vital if schools are to accurately reflect the needs of the pupils and make them feel valued and supported. One of the main findings of the research was that, whilst the pupils felt that teaching was good, many felt that school was not a safe place. On a site originally designed for 700 pupils and now accommodating 1270, many pupils felt threatened and overcrowded.

In response to that information the school has invested a great deal of time and effort in making pupils feel safer, often employing strategies mentioned elsewhere in the book like zoning the school and transmitting clear social values through PSHE/citizenship. Additionally great emphasis has been laid upon making rewards and sanctions a positive process. Parents are kept fully informed and pupils are expected to take an active part in the whole process.

The level of sanctions

The main emphasis of this system is the use of the minimum sanction or a relevant reward to achieve the desired result. Mike

Ford is clear in his view that the use of extreme measures undoubtedly changes behaviour, but often for the worse. By the same token rewards that take the form of 'grand gestures' are hard to sustain. Something simple, on the other hand, like inviting a pupil into the headteacher's or deputy head's office to receive a certificate or to be praised can have a marked effect, particularly on those pupils whose only other visits have been to receive reprimands.

The system at South Bromsgrove offers pupils a choice and sense of responsibility. 'Don't tell them off', says Mike: 'Put them right so that they don't get into trouble with someone else.' 'If the school is a community where pupils should feel a sense of belonging then the management of that community should be based on a sense of partnership.' Staff do not say 'tuck your shirt in', they ask, 'Is it time to get tidied up?', thereby inviting compliance. On matters such as litter the headteacher and deputies, who always spend some part of break and dinner times around the school, pick up litter as they move around. Mike says:

> 'We are always joined and assisted by some pupils. Some never bother, and that is fine but whatever happens the message is there for all to see and those pupils, sometimes the most vulnerable, who want to join us, however briefly, are given the chance to feel valued and part of the community.'

School detention

In keeping with the philosophy of shared responsibility, although there is a whole school code of conduct the practice of operating a whole school detention policy at South Bromsgrove has been discontinued. Under the present system staff continue to keep parents fully informed but, in truth, the generally held view is that letters home rarely have a significant or lasting effect. Through discussion staff concluded that the most important thing was the appropriateness of the sanction. By and large it was felt that staff use punishment for one of three reasons:

- To make them feel better (revenge)
- As an example to others
- To change behaviour

The overwhelming view was that the only valid use of punishment was for the last reason. On that basis the conclusion reached was that blanket punishments were inappropriate if the real intention was to target the behaviour of an individual. Staff at the school now 'negotiate' with pupils when sanctions are imposed. Most staff have times when they remain in school during a lunch hour or after school and it is at those times that pupils are required to carry out some form of 'community service' around the school to make up for misdemeanours. As a result of this system it has become impossible for pupils or parents to refuse punishments due to some difficulty or another. The punishment is simply moved. Pupils are not forced to miss positive aspects of their lives like playing for the school team or attending rehearsals, and staff are not 'punished' by the system because they impose sanctions at their convenience and can choose tasks, like tidying cupboards, that will benefit them and other pupils.

One of the most innovative aspects of the system is the opportunity for pupils to 'earn remission'. Pupils who may be required to report to a teacher for three fifteen minute sessions to serve their punishment can, if they behave positively and carry out tasks adequately on the first two occasions, be excused the third. Through this simple process the sanction really does become a partnership. Teachers have the chance to judge whether behaviour has changed and pupils have the opportunity to show that they wish to correct what has gone before in a manner that will benefit both parties.

Reintegrating pupils

As part of the support systems for pupils, South Bromsgrove run a 'halfway house' for pupils returning after a period of absence, or those who have faced difficulties in the school's mainstream and are in danger of not attending. The centre, called 'Brookside', is now in its third year and is based in what was a caretaker's house. It was established using a one-off grant from central government which supported the establishment of learning support units, and it has subsequently been funded through the school budget.

Currently the staff consists of two part-time teachers who are supported by staff from the main school who come in and out.

Deputies do break duties in the unit with the deliberate intention that pupils have the opportunity to meet senior staff in a different environment. Parents are encouraged to visit the unit and meetings with them and their children can be held in the office accommodation. Admission to the unit it usually by referral through the year heads.

The views of the pupils are extremely positive. Laura, who had been 'wagging it' (playing truant), said she had found lessons hard so she'd gone off with her mates. By her own admission the places she had gone were only worth 'about four out of ten' but school had 'seemed too hard'. In her view Brookside was better. It had given her the chance to 'talk about problems and sort them out' and staff felt that her confidence was returning.

Mike, who had also been missing school, liked Brookside because it had helped him to talk about things and it 'gives you a chance to catch up before you go back to lessons'.

Education welfare and community policing
There has been a concerted policy in Bromsgrove to ensure that welfare agencies and police work closely to improve attendance and reduce the long-term consequences to the local community of high truancy rates. For both WPC Michelle Caldicott, the community beat manager, and Maggie Gower, the Education Welfare Officer, the welfare of the child is paramount. Both speak with one voice when they say that just as the National Health Service would not refuse treatment to a driver on the basis that they had been driving too fast, so poor attendance at school is no reason to withdraw support and assistance from pupils who truant.

That said, both concede that there is a tendency for people to make stereotypical judgements about truants, which are neither accurate nor helpful. The pressure placed on schools by league tables leads them to resent truants and the budgetary constraints and targets placed upon the police and welfare services encourage 'fire bucket management' rather than early intervention and long-term support projects.

Both Maggie and Michelle feel that the way forward is to develop a relationship and an understanding with the truants and their families. Often truancy is a cultural issue. Parents often had attendance problems themselves and see nothing wrong with condoning the occasional absence. Unfortunately they have no appreciation that condoned absence often escalates to truancy and that truancy is significantly connected to issues such as substance abuse and other criminal behaviour.

By the same token absence is a regular thing for some pupils. They feel out of place at school and so congregate with people they know in their own territory, where they feel comfortable. It often comes as a surprise to them that their normal behaviour can be offensive and intimidating to other people.

Maggie and Michelle have invested a lot of time in forging relationships. They organize their hours so that they can visit families and can enter the places frequented by the truants at times they are likely to be there, and are on first name terms with many of them. The questions they most frequently ask are, 'Why are you out of school?' and, 'What can we do to get you back in?'

Both are certain that the existence of the Brookside project is a real asset to their work and feel that the increased development and use of the alternative curriculum, particularly in secondary schools, is the way forward. At present both are involved in extending their multi-agency approach by enlisting the assistance of newly appointed neighbourhood wardens as their 'eyes and ears' in the community.

Connexions

Emma McGettrick and Clare Davies carry out the work of Connexions at South Bromsgrove. In some schools the management expect Connexions to adopt a strictly regimented approach and to carry out counselling, particularly careers advice, following narrow guidelines imposed by the school. South Bromsgrove, however, recognize that Connexions has a wider role and are receptive to the multi-agency approach that Emma, Clare and their organization favour. As well as working in school Emma and Clare have established a lunchtime 'drop-in centre' at the local community centre, where they are joined by a youth worker and a sexual health nurse. The emphasis of their work is early intervention with the target age group of 13–25-year-olds. Of particular interest are those already or likely to become 'not in education employment or training'. This 'NEET' group is of prime concern to the advisors since they are vulnerable at school, are increasingly vulnerable once they have left and lack direction. Regular contact and impartial advice form the basis of all the work that is done by Connexions and great emphasis is placed on Assessment Planning Implementation and Review (APIR).

Emma and Clare are under no illusion about the task that faces them. Keeping children in school and supporting them is of paramount importance, especially in Worcestershire, which has, they say, the highest exclusion rate of any county in England. Although they agree that Connexions is not a panacea, there is evidence that they are making a difference. Like the school in which they work, and in line with other research evidence available in England and Wales, they are convinced that early intervention and a multi-agency approach is the most effective. As well as working with agencies mentioned elsewhere in this book Connexions also provide courses for the alternative curriculum. In South Bromsgrove, as part of Project 19, an alternative curriculum programme, with the support of a teaching assistant and resources paid for by the school, they provide an advisor to deliver the Prince's Trust Excel course.

Additionally, pupils who are in any way vulnerable or in need of support can rely upon them for confidential support in group or one-to-one situations. Pupils lacking direction are offered careers advice, victims of bullying and bullies are counselled and supported and statemented pupils are given transition reviews to ensure that they are achieving their potential and making progress.

The contribution made by Connexions, whether at a parents' evening, on results day or any other time in the school year is designed to support pupils and make them feel valued. There is no doubt that their work is important and if it is integrated into the school in the way it is at South Bromsgrove then it can be a valuable aid to improving attendance and raising achievement. (See Appendix D.)

The Youth Offending Service

The Youth Offending Service (YOS) is the agency primarily responsible for administering supervision orders taken out against young people. Additionally, and amongst its other duties, the service has responsibility for raising awareness in the community with the intention of preventing juvenile crime and raising the sense of well-being in the wider community.

At South Bromsgrove the YOS worker is Ann Mann. Ann has extensive experience in the field of youth justice and welfare and believes in the importance of youth justice as a tool to focus a young person's mind on education and to encourage new approaches and attitudes amongst juveniles. Although not every service takes exactly the same view, Ann lays great store by effective practice and quality assurance research findings which reveal that education is a significant factor in the prevention of re-offending behaviour amongst young people.

By working closely with the school to combat poor attendance Ann believes that the twin targets of raised achievement and reduced juvenile crime can be more easily achieved. It is Ann's view that the current practice of classifying absence as authorized or unauthorized is open to abuse. There is, amongst parents, a mistaken belief that 'so long as they have a letter it's OK'. 'On the basis of that definition', says Ann, 'truancy can start in reception. What parents fail to realize is that by condoning absence they are laying the foundation for behaviour that will lead to truanting.' Whilst it is true that there is no proven link between truancy and offending behaviour, research does demonstrate, 'A high percentage of offenders with school problems in the areas of behaviour, attainment and attendance.' On that basis alone Ann feels there is sufficient reason to support strong links between schools and the YOS.

The YOS and schools

Ann Mann and her coworkers in the Worcestershire and Herefordshire YOS have a strong belief in the significance of education in reducing rates of re-offending. Together with the school the YOS can set up Education Action Plans that take account of such factors as previous attendance patterns and special needs. Pupils can be set 'smart targets' for improving attendance, thereby reducing opportunities to return to offending habits. These targets should be sensible enough to ensure that pupils are not set up to fail but sufficiently supervised to ensure that new habits are formed. Ann tries where possible to arrange supervision appointments to coincide with PSHE lessons and finds that by linking with this area of the curriculum she is more able to ensure a child's attendance. Additionally, the school and the YOS make use of a regional scheme called Euro K.4. Financed by the European Social Fund this scheme targets KS4 pupils and in concert with the various youth support and welfare agencies sets out to address offending behaviour, reduce exclusion and improve attendance.

Deciding to truant

Irrespective of the opinions of teachers and other education support workers, the fact is that those who do not attend school have taken a rational decision. They are choosing not to attend school in order to be in a situation where they (the truant) believe they are deriving greater benefit. Often, given the number found with parents on truancy sweeps, that decision is taken with the full knowledge of the parent. What the school and the EWS must do is convince parents and pupils that they still have a choice and that the benefits associated with attendance are greater than those that might be derived from choosing absence.

Dads and Lads programmes

In the UK 83 per cent of those excluded from school are boys, and research evidence has made it abundantly clear that excluded pupils are more likely to have continuing difficulties at school, to be poor attenders, and to become involved in some sort of offending behaviour.

Six years ago YMCA England launched an innovative scheme called 'Dads and Lads.' Using sport as its starting point the project set out to enhance positive interaction and communication between fathers and their sons by setting up projects where they could meet to discuss and develop common interests.

Explaining the need for such an initiative Mark Chester, Dads and Lads Development Worker for YMCA England, says:

'Studies have shown that by sharing activities with their sons fathers can positively influence self-esteem, educational achievement and social skills. However, living under the same roof does not guarantee involvement which is where this scheme comes in.'

Projects can be set up with the support of the YMCA for as little as £50 and are operated all over the country by schools, local authorities, community groups and professional sports clubs. In addition to sport, projects now offer activities such as reading, creative writing, cooking, kite-making and rocket-building and in some areas the projects have been extended and are now called 'Dads, Lads and Lasses'.

Some facts
- Having a committed father makes the second biggest difference after social class.
- The reading score of a seven-year-old boy is 20 per cent higher if his father reads with him.
- In families where fathers show kindness, care and warmth during primary school years, children are more likely to do well at secondary school.
- The involvement of the father at the age of 7–11 has been shown to influence the number of examination passes at the age of 16.
- Children whose fathers are involved with them before the age of 11 are more likely to avoid having a criminal record by the age of 21.

These facts and the report from which they are taken, 'Fatherfacts', can be downloaded from www.fathersdirect.com.

Alternative courses

Around they country there are numerous different approaches to the alternative curriculum, catering for children from the point of admission in reception classes to those pupils whose education is provided in a special school or a pupil referral unit. Despite their diversity, however, all of these alternative courses have one thing in common. They all take the view that:

If the child can't learn in the way that we teach them then we must teach them in the way in which they learn.

The British government's policy of increased flexibility has made the idea of diversity within the curriculum a more realistic option. Now that schools have increased powers to 'disapply' pupils from the National Curriculum, many schools are taking the opportunity to devise courses that more accurately meet the needs of pupils who have specific difficulties which create a barrier to learning and might result in truancy.

ASDAN

Based in Bristol, the Awards Scheme and Accreditation Network is at the forefront of developing alternative courses which either augment the existing curriculum or replace it with courses that are more relevant to the particular needs of pupils. Those courses that augment the curriculum offer enrichment to pupils at all levels by offering opportunities to raise self-awareness and self-esteem, whilst those that are designed to replace the normal curriculum offer new learning and achievement opportunities to pupils who, for whatever reason, have found it hard to access the mainstream curriculum.

Courses are classified as bronze, silver or gold according to their content and cover a variety of vocational sporting and community-based topics as well as incorporating key skills at a level appropriate to the course content. Gold awards are already recognised by UCAS (Universities Central Admissions System) as part of the qualification process for university, and from September 2004 other courses now have a direct equivalence to others in the National Qualifications Framework. In consequence schools will be able to encourage attendance by offering different courses and the results will, for the first time, contribute to the school's achievement statistics.

The Prince's Trust

The Prince's Trust is the UK's leading charity for young people, and since 1976 over 475,000 people between the ages of 14 and 30 have benefitted from its core programmes. Of particular interest to schools operating an alternative curriculum are programmes such as the Youth Achievement Awards, which set challenges for young people through which they can develop personal qualities, interpersonal skills and self-esteem.

XL clubs

This team-based programme of personal development is designed for students in their last two years of compulsory schooling. Currently around 800 clubs in the UK help young people facing difficulties in school, including those with attendance problems or those at risk of exclusion. The XL Award is accredited by ASDAN and gives participants an award in the 'Wider Key Skills' of problem-solving, working with others and improving own learning as well as recognizing achievement in areas such as entrepreneurial skills and citizenship.

The intention is to improve the self-esteem of all team members; to increase the likelihood that they will complete compulsory schooling by enhancing their behaviour and personal skills; to give them the opportunity to attempt qualifications; to enhance their record of achievement; and to equip them more fully to enter the world of work or to embark on further training. At present about 515 UK schools are involved in the project, and since 1999 over 9000 young people have participated.

Bespoke courses

Whilst not every school has introduced courses through ASDAN or the Prince's Trust, a large number, in response to the British Government's call for personalized learning, have formed links with their local FE college in order to provide vocational courses. Warrington Collegiate in Cheshire is one such college. Currently pupils from all the local high schools follow a variety of courses rather than studying full-time at their respective schools. Some of the courses offered are based upon vocational GCSEs but more traditional vocational bodies such as City and Guilds validate others.

The style of courses followed varies from school to school. In some schools the pupils follow courses predominantly based upon the mainstream whilst others follow entirely separate courses that incorporate vocational study, practical college courses and work experience elements. Whatever the format, all of the courses are designed to maintain pupils' interest in school, to ensure that they have the best possible opportunity to complete their education and to give them an opportunity to achieve success in their chosen areas.

Paul Gould, Head of Construction Training at the Collegiate, is in no doubt about the value of the courses and readily quotes examples of pupils who have found new confidence and direction as a result of their experience in the different subject areas. Paul is equally convinced that the pupils who derive the most benefit from such courses are from the schools who provide the greatest support. He says:

> 'There is no doubt that pupils recognize the time and effort that is invested on their behalf. When a school spends time developing strong links with the college, pupils feel valued and their performance improves.'

Conclusion

Given the diversity of the problem it is unsurprising that there should be such a range of different approaches that can be used to support attendance. Clearly, it is impossible to say that one system is better than another or that a particular combination of strategies will always bring results. However, there are common threads in many of the examples given, and underpinning all of them is a belief in the importance of the child.

In the author's own experience of working with pupils following an alternative curriculum it has always been of paramount importance that pupils should feel the positive aspects of such courses and that their parents are fully involved from the outset. Irrespective of the day-to-day inconvenience caused by a pupil's absence they are still worthy of the same support that we would offer to more compliant pupils. Indeed, given the difficulties faced by some poor attenders one might argue that they were deserving of more.

If schools are to succeed in improving attendance then the pupils whose behaviour they seek to modify must feel wanted. An alternative curriculum course must be offered as an opportunity and pupils must not feel that it is a backwater where they have been discarded. Schools that try to subsidize the education of the 'good children' by supporting children with problems 'on the cheap' are wasting their time and their money. Such a course of action serves only to reinforce the sense of alienation already felt by poor attenders and ignores the moral remit of the educator to reach out and make a difference to every pupil.

10 What the Buggers Said

This last section, although brief, is given over entirely to some of those interviewed by the author and whose well-being is central to this book. The last word is theirs.

Pupils interviewed saw personal safety and the making of rules at all levels as likely causes of truancy in all its forms. A sense of identity with the school was important in preventing truancy, as was (less frequently) the fear of getting caught. The point at which fear as a preventative measure operated varied radically. At one extreme was the pupil who declared, 'I'd never do it, you only get caught and my mum would kill me.' At the other extreme was another child who had just returned to school after persistent truancy, which had often been condoned by the parents. In this case only a court case and a threat of local authority care had forced a return to school.

The reason offered most frequently by children for truancy was boredom. Naturally the definition of boredom varied, though a number of children agreed that having played truant they discovered that this too was boring.

There was a general tendency amongst those interviewed to make general assumptions from specific experiences. Once they had become disenchanted with school it was easy for them to feel that if one lesson was bad they were all bad, and if one teacher seemed unreasonable then they all were. At the same time and paradoxically there were two pupils who said independently of each other that they 'had nothing against school they just didn't like going'.

Some Quotes

'Some lessons are good, some lessons are bad. Mostly it's OK.'

'I think even the teachers are bored in some lessons.'

'Teachers should share jokes and not be "narky" all the time.'

'Teachers think they are right and even if you tell them it's not you they won't listen, even when you are telling them the truth.'

'I like music lessons and the tuckshop. School makes you feel welcome.'

'I'd never tell a teacher.'

'Sometimes you should tell if something's really important like bullying or something.'

'The best things are PE, music, drama club, trips and home time.'

'School's good. You'd have no friends if you stayed at home.'

'They stop bullying at our school so it's OK.'

'Once I nicked off and it was boring and I banged my head on the bridge where we hid.'

'The toilets stink but it's better than [name of lesson].'

'Racism.'

'I hate when you can't do the lessons and the more clever ones pick on you and make fun.'

'When you're being blamed for something you haven't done, or when teachers pick on you they won't even listen and neither will your mum and dad when they tell them.'

'It's not fair when you do something little but the teacher goes really mad and you get really done but you know it's just him and it doesn't really matter.'

'It's rotten when you get a reputation and they say "you again". After that when they catch you its always you even when it isn't.'

'They tell us to respect them then they treat us like s**t.'

One pupil who was anxious to express a view and clearly held his opinion with sincerity said he had played truant for 'personal reasons' and 'no one had the right to know why'. He refused to give any explanation of his absence and whilst one could not condone his behaviour one felt sympathy with this assertion that: 'Grown ups and teachers have private reasons and so have I.'

And Finally . . .

'Teachers should go on a course for handling kids.'

Appendix A

Pupil Absence in Maintained Primary and Secondary Schools in England in 2002/2003: Revised Statistics

Local Education Authority	All Schools[1]			Primary Schools			Secondary Schools		
	Total Absence	Authorized Absence	Unauthorized Absence	Total Absence	Authorized Absence	Unauthorized Absence	Total Absence	Authorized Absence	Unauthorized Absence
Barking and Dagenham	7.89	6.29	1.60	6.74	5.38	1.37	9.44	7.53	1.91
Barnet	6.50	5.75	0.74	5.79	5.23	0.56	7.37	6.39	0.97
Barnsley	7.92	6.90	1.02	6.69	5.94	0.75	9.50	8.12	1.38
Bath and North East Somerset	6.60	6.02	0.57	5.15	4.83	0.32	8.03	7.21	0.83
Bedfordshire	6.44	6.09	0.34	5.53	5.32	0.21	6.98	6.56	0.42
Bexley	7.02	6.48	0.54	6.15	5.80	0.35	8.01	7.26	0.75
Birmingham	7.64	6.63	1.02	6.84	6.19	0.65	8.68	7.18	1.50
Blackburn with Darwen	7.43	6.64	0.79	6.45	6.00	0.45	8.80	7.54	1.26
Blackpool	8.02	7.04	0.98	6.61	5.93	0.68	9.90	8.54	1.37
Bolton	6.60	5.89	0.71	5.22	4.89	0.33	8.18	7.04	1.14
Bournemouth	6.63	6.23	0.39	5.38	5.18	0.20	7.91	7.32	0.59
Bracknell Forest	6.20	5.76	0.43	5.15	5.00	0.15	7.78	6.91	0.87
Bradford	7.37	5.85	1.52	5.72	5.03	0.69	9.58	6.95	2.63
Brent	7.11	6.51	0.60	6.23	5.82	0.41	8.30	7.43	0.86
Brighton and Hove	7.85	6.88	0.96	6.98	6.43	0.55	8.93	7.45	1.47
Bristol, City of	8.68	7.31	1.37	7.12	6.19	0.93	11.09	9.04	2.05
Bromley	6.90	6.17	0.73	5.70	5.27	0.43	8.33	7.24	1.09
Buckinghamshire	5.74	5.30	0.44	4.96	4.69	0.27	6.70	6.05	0.65
Bury	6.23	5.76	0.47	5.03	4.76	0.28	7.64	6.94	0.70
Calderdale	6.38	5.86	0.52	5.12	4.81	0.31	7.90	7.13	0.77
Cambridgeshire	6.67	6.13	0.54	5.67	5.33	0.34	7.97	7.16	0.81

Camden	8.45	7.31	1.14	7.53	6.77	0.77	9.55	7.97	1.58
Cheshire	6.07	5.47	0.60	4.82	4.45	0.38	7.54	6.66	0.87
Cornwall	7.18	6.78	0.39	6.03	5.72	0.30	8.50	8.00	0.50
Coventry	7.66	7.08	0.57	6.28	6.06	0.22	9.32	8.32	1.00
Croydon	7.57	6.71	0.87	6.59	5.90	0.69	8.92	7.81	1.10
Cumbria	6.25	5.75	0.49	5.07	4.86	0.21	7.61	6.79	0.82
Darlington	7.69	7.10	0.59	6.38	6.19	0.18	9.22	8.15	1.07
Derby City	7.33	6.44	0.89	6.18	5.57	0.61	8.81	7.55	1.25
Derbyshire	6.64	5.98	0.66	5.57	5.16	0.41	7.95	6.99	0.96
Devon	6.86	6.26	0.59	5.49	5.24	0.25	8.59	7.56	1.03
Doncaster	7.73	6.79	0.94	6.37	5.97	0.40	9.35	7.77	1.58
Dorset	6.52	6.15	0.38	5.39	5.13	0.25	7.42	6.94	0.48
Dudley	7.20	6.61	0.59	6.33	5.97	0.37	8.24	7.38	0.86
Durham	7.20	6.84	0.37	6.04	5.95	0.10	8.60	7.91	0.69
Ealing	6.87	6.38	0.49	6.07	5.84	0.22	8.04	7.16	0.87
East Riding of Yorkshire	6.49	6.06	0.43	5.37	5.18	0.19	7.73	7.04	0.69
East Sussex	6.95	6.12	0.83	5.75	5.34	0.41	8.43	7.08	1.35
Enfield	7.62	6.19	1.44	6.56	5.45	1.11	8.96	7.10	1.85
Essex	6.89	6.31	0.58	5.89	5.52	0.37	8.09	7.25	0.84
Gateshead	6.92	6.35	0.57	5.64	5.38	0.26	8.60	7.63	0.97
Gloucestershire	6.26	5.90	0.36	5.19	4.95	0.24	7.49	6.97	0.51
Greenwich	8.27	6.42	1.85	6.88	5.43	1.45	10.10	7.73	2.37
Hackney	7.89	6.27	1.62	7.26	5.90	1.36	8.99	6.92	2.07
Halton	7.75	6.48	1.27	5.82	5.36	0.46	10.05	7.81	2.24
Hammersmith and Fulham	7.85	6.66	1.19	6.92	6.16	0.76	8.94	7.25	1.69
Hampshire	6.24	5.58	0.66	5.07	4.74	0.33	7.68	6.62	1.07

Local Education Authority	All Schools[1]			Primary Schools			Secondary Schools		
	Total Absence	Authorized Absence	Unauthorized Absence	Total Absence	Authorized Absence	Unauthorized Absence	Total Absence	Authorized Absence	Unauthorized Absence
Haringey	8.25	6.50	1.75	7.34	5.95	1.39	9.68	7.37	2.32
Harrow	6.62	6.30	0.32	6.05	5.83	0.21	7.68	7.16	0.52
Hartlepool	6.81	5.60	1.20	5.53	4.73	0.80	8.36	6.67	1.69
Havering	6.97	6.58	0.39	6.07	5.83	0.24	7.97	7.41	0.56
Herefordshire	6.35	5.88	0.47	5.50	5.31	0.19	7.38	6.58	0.80
Hertfordshire	6.26	5.74	0.53	5.24	4.90	0.34	7.48	6.73	0.75
Hillingdon	7.65	6.55	1.10	6.70	6.02	0.67	8.83	7.20	1.63
Hounslow	7.06	5.95	1.11	6.42	5.23	1.19	7.77	6.74	1.02
Isle of Wight	7.57	6.99	0.59	5.78	5.66	0.12	8.57	7.72	0.85
Isles of Scilly	6.47	5.77	0.70	6.47	5.77	0.70	–	–	–
Islington	8.04	6.69	1.36	7.34	6.08	1.26	9.20	7.69	1.51
Kensington and Chelsea	6.93	5.96	0.97	6.64	6.06	0.59	7.45	5.78	1.66
Kent	6.75	6.24	0.51	5.69	5.32	0.37	8.01	7.35	0.67
Kingston upon Hull, City of	8.78	7.31	1.46	6.59	5.93	0.65	11.41	8.97	2.44
Kingston upon Thames	6.26	5.91	0.35	5.34	5.13	0.22	7.38	6.87	0.51
Kirklees	6.63	5.86	0.77	5.66	5.24	0.41	7.78	6.60	1.19
Knowsley	8.54	6.95	1.59	6.45	5.81	0.64	11.30	8.46	2.84
Lambeth	6.95	6.03	0.92	6.55	5.48	1.07	7.82	7.22	0.60
Lancashire	6.47	5.92	0.54	5.18	4.88	0.31	7.98	7.15	0.82
Leeds	7.47	6.37	1.10	5.88	5.45	0.43	9.41	7.48	1.92
Leicester City	8.03	6.49	1.53	6.81	6.10	0.71	9.59	7.00	2.59
Leicestershire	6.40	5.74	0.66	5.29	5.13	0.17	7.61	6.42	1.19

Lewisham	7.41	5.85	1.57	6.59	5.53	1.06	8.73	6.35	2.38
Lincolnshire	6.45	5.94	0.51	5.43	5.15	0.28	7.63	6.85	0.78
Liverpool	8.34	7.28	1.06	6.60	6.08	0.52	10.33	8.65	1.68
London, City of	5.34	–	–	5.34	5.34	0.00	–	–	–
Luton	7.52	6.88	0.64	6.75	6.22	0.53	8.52	7.73	0.79
Manchester	8.65	7.45	1.19	6.87	6.04	0.83	11.03	9.35	1.68
Medway	7.00	6.48	0.52	5.92	5.62	0.30	8.24	7.47	0.77
Merton	7.20	6.43	0.77	6.07	5.72	0.35	8.75	7.40	1.34
Middlesbrough	8.14	7.46	0.68	6.65	6.28	0.37	10.19	9.08	1.11
Milton Keynes	6.76	6.32	0.44	5.75	5.46	0.29	8.58	7.88	0.71
Newcastle upon Tyne	8.10	7.22	0.88	6.35	5.86	0.49	9.87	8.60	1.27
Newham	6.37	5.08	1.29	5.98	4.94	1.04	6.86	5.26	1.60
Norfolk	7.35	6.66	0.69	6.12	5.67	0.45	9.07	8.05	1.02
North East Lincolnshire	7.76	6.83	0.93	5.75	5.53	0.23	10.00	8.29	1.72
North Lincolnshire	6.92	6.37	0.55	5.77	5.54	0.22	8.19	7.29	0.91
North Somerset	6.79	6.09	0.69	5.57	5.26	0.31	8.16	7.03	1.13
North Tyneside	6.53	6.05	0.48	5.37	5.25	0.12	7.74	6.88	0.86
North Yorkshire	6.00	5.65	0.35	4.82	4.67	0.16	7.31	6.74	0.57
Northamptonshire	7.02	6.30	0.72	5.50	5.11	0.39	8.71	7.63	1.08
Northumberland	6.82	6.53	0.29	5.69	5.50	0.19	7.43	7.09	0.34
Nottingham City	8.15	6.81	1.34	6.55	5.85	0.70	10.73	8.36	2.37
Nottinghamshire	7.13	6.23	0.90	5.95	5.55	0.39	8.50	7.02	1.49
Oldham	7.41	6.45	0.96	6.05	5.59	0.46	9.02	7.47	1.55
Oxfordshire	6.35	5.69	0.66	5.19	4.91	0.29	7.66	6.57	1.09
Peterborough City	7.03	6.35	0.68	6.08	5.56	0.51	8.18	7.29	0.89
Plymouth	7.06	6.64	0.42	5.97	5.72	0.26	8.22	7.63	0.59

Local Education Authority	All Schools[1]			Primary Schools			Secondary Schools		
	Total Absence	Authorized Absence	Unauthorized Absence	Total Absence	Authorized Absence	Unauthorized Absence	Total Absence	Authorized Absence	Unauthorized Absence
Poole	6.50	5.83	0.67	5.52	5.05	0.47	7.82	6.87	0.94
Portsmouth	7.61	6.53	1.08	6.01	5.19	0.82	9.61	8.19	1.42
Reading	7.29	6.27	1.02	6.12	5.69	0.43	9.22	7.23	1.99
Redbridge	6.36	5.63	0.73	6.18	5.41	0.77	6.58	5.89	0.69
Redcar and Cleveland	6.97	6.38	0.60	5.67	5.43	0.25	8.35	7.38	0.97
Richmond upon Thames	6.63	5.54	1.09	5.08	4.76	0.32	8.67	6.57	2.10
Rochdale	7.30	6.35	0.95	5.92	5.35	0.57	8.99	7.58	1.41
Rotherham	7.30	6.45	0.84	6.18	5.71	0.46	8.56	7.29	1.27
Rutland	5.60	5.27	0.32	4.63	4.48	0.15	6.56	6.07	0.49
Salford	8.21	7.02	1.19	6.26	5.82	0.43	10.81	8.62	2.19
Sandwell	8.66	7.71	0.95	7.11	6.64	0.47	10.64	9.07	1.56
Sefton	6.69	6.26	0.43	5.68	5.46	0.22	7.81	7.14	0.67
Sheffield	7.67	6.40	1.27	6.11	5.45	0.66	9.60	7.58	2.02
Shropshire	6.23	5.95	0.28	5.39	5.25	0.13	7.19	6.73	0.46
Slough	7.10	6.04	1.06	6.83	6.08	0.75	7.44	5.98	1.46
Solihull	6.25	5.70	0.55	5.15	4.84	0.31	7.49	6.67	0.82
Somerset	6.65	6.21	0.45	5.51	5.24	0.27	7.87	7.24	0.63
South Gloucestershire	6.65	5.96	0.69	5.36	5.08	0.27	8.38	7.14	1.25
South Tyneside	7.20	6.80	0.40	5.79	5.63	0.15	8.90	8.21	0.69
Southampton	7.91	7.05	0.86	6.76	6.16	0.60	9.31	8.13	1.18
Southend-on-Sea	7.16	6.23	0.94	6.09	5.49	0.60	8.45	7.11	1.34
Southwark	7.26	5.50	1.75	6.63	4.89	1.74	8.43	6.64	1.79

St Helens	6.99	6.29	0.70	5.72	5.38	0.35	8.52	7.40	1.13
Staffordshire	6.38	5.94	0.44	5.35	5.13	0.22	7.42	6.76	0.66
Stockport	6.28	5.73	0.54	5.23	4.92	0.31	7.55	6.72	0.82
Stockton on Tees	6.74	6.29	0.45	5.65	5.44	0.21	7.99	7.27	0.72
Stoke on Trent	7.32	6.23	1.10	6.38	5.64	0.74	8.39	6.88	1.50
Suffolk	6.55	5.84	0.71	5.07	4.81	0.25	7.74	6.66	1.08
Sunderland	7.38	6.86	0.52	6.03	5.84	0.18	8.94	8.03	0.90
Surrey	6.39	5.80	0.59	5.35	5.06	0.29	7.75	6.77	0.98
Sutton	6.15	5.69	0.46	5.57	5.31	0.26	6.72	6.07	0.66
Swindon	6.15	5.75	0.41	5.21	5.01	0.20	7.37	6.70	0.67
Tameside	6.91	6.52	0.39	5.89	5.53	0.36	8.03	7.59	0.43
Telford and Wrekin	6.90	6.53	0.38	5.94	5.68	0.27	8.13	7.61	0.51
Thurrock	7.64	6.65	0.99	6.78	6.25	0.53	8.80	7.18	1.62
Torbay	7.12	6.24	0.88	5.77	5.44	0.34	8.65	7.16	1.49
Tower Hamlets	7.32	5.76	1.56	6.62	5.43	1.20	8.24	6.21	2.03
Trafford	5.70	5.32	0.38	4.76	4.59	0.17	6.70	6.10	0.60
Wakefield	7.13	6.38	0.75	6.01	5.45	0.55	8.48	7.48	1.00
Walsall	7.80	7.14	0.66	6.68	6.20	0.47	9.02	8.17	0.86
Waltham Forest	7.05	6.14	0.90	6.35	5.81	0.54	7.94	6.57	1.37
Wandsworth	7.21	6.43	0.78	6.42	5.84	0.58	8.42	7.33	1.09
Warrington	5.89	5.41	0.47	4.80	4.47	0.33	7.23	6.58	0.65
Warwickshire	6.37	5.91	0.46	5.32	5.12	0.20	7.60	6.84	0.76
West Berkshire	6.29	5.83	0.46	5.15	4.84	0.30	7.44	6.83	0.61
West Sussex	6.60	6.13	0.47	5.45	5.20	0.25	8.10	7.35	0.75
Westminster, City of	7.11	6.04	1.08	6.22	5.60	0.62	8.14	6.54	1.59
Wigan	6.65	6.24	0.41	5.55	5.30	0.25	7.91	7.31	0.60

Local Education Authority	All Schools[1]			Primary Schools			Secondary Schools		
	Total Absence	Authorized Absence	Unauthorized Absence	Total Absence	Authorized Absence	Unauthorized Absence	Total Absence	Authorized Absence	Unauthorized Absence
Wiltshire	6.35	5.91	0.44	5.12	4.82	0.30	7.83	7.23	0.60
Windsor & Maidenhead	6.11	5.56	0.55	4.84	4.50	0.34	7.19	6.47	0.72
Wirral	6.57	6.11	0.47	5.49	5.08	0.41	7.76	7.22	0.54
Wokingham	5.96	5.56	0.40	4.74	4.55	0.20	7.31	6.69	0.62
Wolverhampton	7.70	6.90	0.80	6.82	6.33	0.49	8.84	7.64	1.20
Worcestershire	6.63	6.14	0.50	5.44	5.25	0.19	7.65	6.89	0.76
York, City of	6.43	5.67	0.76	5.29	4.84	0.45	7.82	6.67	1.14
Total[2] (Maintained schools only)	6.94	6.22	0.72	5.81	5.38	0.43	8.28	7.21	1.07
ENGLAND[3]	6.83	6.13	0.70						

1. Includes maintained primary and secondary schools only. Figures rounded up.
2. The figures by LEA relate to maintained primary and secondary schools including academies, but excluding maintained special schools and CTCs.
3. The England figure relates to all schools in England including special schools and independent schools and cannot be broken down into primary and secondary because of the overlap.

Appendix B

HMYOI Thorn Cross: Research Questionnaire

1. Inmate Number _____

2. Age _____

3. What was your offence? *(Please tick a box)*

   Car related   ☐

   Violence   ☐

   Theft   ☐

   Drugs   ☐

   Burglary   ☐

   Other *(Please explain)* _____

4. Did you commit your crimes after taking drugs or alcohol?

   Yes ☐   No ☐

5. Length of sentence *(please tick a box)*

   0–3 months ☐   4–6 months ☐   7–9 months ☐

   10–12 months ☐   13–18 months ☐   19–24 months ☐

   Longer than 24 months ☐ *(say how long)* _____

6. How long do you expect to serve? _____

7. Including this time, how many times you have been convicted?

   Once ☐   Twice ☐   Three Times ☐   Four Times ☐

   More than four times ☐ *(say how many)* _____

8. How many times have you been in prison?

   Once ☐   Twice ☐   Three Times ☐   Four Times ☐

   More than four times ☐ *(say how many)*_____

9. Including this sentence what is the total time *(in years and months)* that you have been sentenced to by the courts?

   _____ Years   _____ Months

10. Including this sentence what is the total of the time you have spent in prison?

    _____ Years   _____ Months

11. When convicted did you have any similar offences taken into consideration?

    Yes ☐   No ☐

    If you answered yes, how many offences were taken into consideration?

    _____

School History

12. How many infant schools (age 4–7) did you attend?
    (Please tick a box)

    1 ☐ 2 ☐ 3 ☐ 4 ☐ More than 4 ☐ *(say how many)*_____

13. How many junior schools (age 8–11) did you attend?
    (Please tick a box)

    1 ☐ 2 ☐ 3 ☐ 4 ☐ More than 4 ☐ *(say how many)*_____

14. How many secondary schools (age 11–16) did you attend?
    (Please tick a box)

    1 ☐ 2 ☐ 3 ☐ 4 ☐ More than 4 ☐ *(say how many)*_____

15. If you went to more than one school please give your reasons below.
    (Please tick the box next to the reasons)

    Moved House ☐   How many times? ☐

Left due to problems *(e.g. Bullying, unhappiness)* ☐
How many times? ☐

Moved to take a more appropriate course ☐
How many times? ☐

Imprisoned ☐   How many times? ☐

Thrown out of school ☐   How many times? ☐

Other *(please explain and give number of times)*

_____

16. Did you ever play truant from school? *(Tick a box)*

Never ☐   Every day ☐   Once a week ☐

Once a month ☐   Once a term ☐

Once every six months ☐   Once a year ☐

Less than once a year ☐

17. Did you ever truant without being caught by your parents?

Sometimes ☐   Always ☐   Never ☐

18. Did you ever truant without being caught by your teachers?

Sometimes ☐   Always ☐   Never ☐

19. Did you ever stay off school when you weren't ill with the knowledge and/or agreement of your parents?

Sometimes ☐   Often ☐   Always ☐   Never ☐

20. Why did you truant from school? *(Tick a box)*

Boredom ☐   Fear for your own safety ☐

To avoid trouble with teachers ☐   To be with friends ☐

To commit crime ☐

Other *(please explain)* _____

21. Were you thrown out of school for not attending?

Yes ☐   No ☐

22. Were your first crimes committed before or after leaving school at age 16?

Before ☐   After ☐

23. Did you ever commit crime whilst truanting?

Sometimes ☐   Often ☐   Always ☐   Never ☐

24. Did you complete your full-time education? *(Leaving at 16 with the other people in your year)*

Yes ☐   No ☐

25. If your answer to question 24 is no, please explain why you left before completing your education.

_____

26. What qualifications did you gain before leaving school? *(Tick one box)*

5 or more GCSE's at grade C or above ☐

1 ☐ 2 ☐ 3 ☐ or 4 ☐ GCSEs at grade C or above *(tick one box)*

1 ☐ 2 ☐ 3 ☐ or 4 ☐ GCSEs below grade C *(tick one box)*

5 or more GCSE's below grade C ☐

No qualifications ☐

Other Qualifications *(please specify)* _____

27. Since leaving school have you had any paid employment?

Yes ☐   No ☐

28. If the answer to 27 is yes please give the job titles and the approximate time you spent working there.

_____

29. Since leaving school have you taken part in any training schemes such as the Prince's Trust or the YMCA?

No ☐   Yes ☐   *(please say what you did)*

_____

30. If you have anything else you want to say please use the space below. *Thank you for your cooperation and help.*

_____

_____

_____

_____

_____

_____

_____

_____

_____

_____

Appendix C

Support Agencies and Resources Offering Help to Additional Language and Asylum Seeker Families

- 'Aiming High' – 'Understanding the Educational Needs of Ethnic Minority Pupils in Mainly White Schools.' British Government Initiative. DfES reference: DfES/0416/2004.
- Citizenship Materials: Secondary–Aegis Trust. www.chantelle.lee@aegistrust.org.
- *Home from Home: A guidance and resource pack for the welcome and inclusion of refugee families and children in schools.* Bill Bolton (ed.), 2003. Save the Children.
- Primary/Secondary Refugee Week. Free training, free materials. www.sarah.clay@refugee council.org.uk.
- Refugee Council. Free booklets in different languages explaining the school system in different regions of the British Isles. www.refugeecouncil.org.

Appendix D

Connexions Guidelines

Dear Colleague

Connexions and Education Welfare Services: Working Together to Tackle Truancy

It is clear that the people working in Local Education Authority Education Welfare Services and the Connexions service both have a key role in combating disaffection and promoting regular school attendance for young people. All Connexions Partnerships are signed up to contributing to reducing truancy as part of their work to reduce the number of young people not in education, employment or training, and thereby complementing the work of Education Welfare Services in this area.

Tackling truancy is high on the British Government's agenda to raise standards in education, with a Public Service Agreement to reduce school truancies by 10 per cent by 2004 compared to 2002, sustain the new lower level, and improve overall attendance levels thereafter.

This Summer [2003] a group of expert practitioners from Connexions and Education Welfare Services met to look at how best people can work together in order to be effective in addressing school attendance issues both at a strategic level and in schools.

One outcome of the meeting was the attached list of key actions to promote good practice between Education Welfare Service and Connexions. The intention of the document is to provide a helpful starting point for discussion between personnel from Connexions and Education Welfare Service in order to clarify roles and establish protocols for joint working with the overall aim of making an impact on school attendance.

Christopher Connolly
School Attendance Team
DfES
Sanctuary Buildings
Great Smith Street
London, SW1P 3BT

Tel 020 7925 6150

Connexions and Education Welfare Services: Working Together to Tackle Truancy

1. Local Connexions Partnerships and local Education Welfare Services (EWS) agree their respective roles and responsibilities in relation to attendance issues.
2. Connexions and EWS agree how they are going to work with each other to tackle truancy.
3. Connexions and EWS agree reciprocal representation on relevant strategic management and steering groups.
4. Connexions and EWS consider locating Personnel Advisers (PAs) and Education Welfare Officers (EWOs) in the same premises to promote joined-up working.
5. Connexions and EWS identify opportunities for secondments and/or job shadowing between Connexions and EWS and vice versa so that PAs and EWOs are able to gain a clearer understanding of each others' roles and responsibilities.
6. Connexions and EWS identify and provide opportunities for joint training of PAs and EWOs.
7. The focus for support personnel to be seen by young people as supportive rather than punitive.
8. Ideally Connexions and EWS use and have access to a single database and should share data when dealing with attendance.
9. Connexions and EWS clearly explain, communicate and promote their roles and responsibilities to schools and other organizations. Connexions and EWS are transparent about their relationship with key partners and are specific about the support they are able to provide them.
10. There is a consistency of planning from the LEA to school to pupil level.
11. LEAs work with headteachers so that higher level targets on attendance become the focus of their attention and this is

demonstrated through the targets set in school improvement plans, the EDP.

12. Connexions and EWS feed into the work being carried out on school behaviour and attendance audits and staff training by KS3 consultants as part of the KSZ Behaviour and Attendance Programme rolling out to all secondary schools.

13. Connexions Partnership agreements with schools reflect school level targets for attendance.

14. Connexions Partnerships use attendance rates as an indicator in the allocation of resources to schools.

15. Connexions and the EWS work with schools to agree mechanisms for identifying risk factors that may lead to non-attendance and the mechanisms by which social inclusion teams and Connexions PAs will be notified of those pupils who are at risk.

16. Connexions, EWS and schools agree criteria for dealing with non-attendance which specify the intervention that should take place and the organization responsible for dealing with it at any specified level.

17. Connexions and EWS staff carry out joint home visits to non-attending pupils to pick up complementary areas of pupil need.

18. Connexions and EWS work together in developing good practice for identifying the levels of need and support of young people.

19. Connexions, EWS and other relevant agencies form a core group to focus on the issue of truancy. The organizations represented on the group agree joint protocols about how they will work together on encouraging those who are disengaged from school to return to mainstream schooling.

20. Connexions, EWS and other agencies work together on follow up action after truancy sweeps.

21. Young people should be involved in systems designed to engage them in learning in order to strengthen their role.

22. Connexions, EWS and other relevant agencies work together on improving alternative provision for those for whom return to mainstream school is inappropriate.

23. Regular reviews of local practice take place to see what is effective and what is not working.

Index